50 ideal

Bible

Puppet Scripts

For All Ages

Written by

Peter Hellyer

50 Ideal Bible Puppet Scripts For All Ages
Written by Peter Hellyer
Edited by Harry Barrett

ISBN 1-904172-04-0

A One Way UK Publication
First Published in Great Britain 2002

One Way UK Creative Ministries
Ice House Christian Centre
Victor Street
Grimsby
DN32 7QN

Sales Department: 01472 362810
Training Department: 01472 241068
Email: info@onewayuk.com
Website: www.onewayuk.com

Introduction

A message from the author

The scripts in this book have been especially written to provide a variety of approaches and subjects for both use within and outside the Church. ***The collection is ideal for those starting off in puppetry as well as for those in established teams.***

Copying the scripts

As purchaser of this book, the publisher, One Way UK, gives permission for you to use the scripts for any non-profit making performance. In addition, you may also photocopy any of the scripts for the use of puppeteers working with you on a performance. However, we do ask that the copies made are either destroyed at the end of the performance or returned to you as owner of the book. If the book is purchased on behalf of a church or puppet team, any copies made should be destroyed once used, or retained with the book by the person responsible for puppet performances. Copies may not be made for any other purpose. You may record the scripts for your own personal performance use only. The reproduction of such recordings would infringe copyright.

Adaptation of skits

You may change names that have been used within scripts, for either characters or locations, to fit your own circumstances. The author and publisher wish you to treat the book as your resource.

Appropriate audiences

We do not believe puppets are "only for children" and many of the sketches will be found to have a wide appeal. Puppets can be used in many different circumstances. Puppeteers associated with One Way UK have used puppets in schools of all types, care homes, churches of all denominations, prisons, shopping precincts and other open-air venues. They have also used puppets in a variety of different cultures at home and overseas.

Staging

A conventional puppet stage is all that is required to perform the scripts. Scripts are included that feature animal puppets. So, if you have been wondering what to do with the camels, rabbits, donkeys, sheep and cows you have bought you may well find some answers within this collection!

Puppetry resources

Please remember that One Way UK stock many creative resources designed to help you in your puppetry. These include puppets, staging and accessories, as well as a range of specialist guides. Remember to find out about the training days run by One Way UK either from their website www.onewayuk.com or from their headquarters in Grimsby.

We have a great God and it is the vision of all those associated with One Way UK Creative Ministries to see the very highest quality of puppetry used in His service.

A great deal of thought has gone into creating this book. It is hoped that the result will prove a blessing to your ministry. If you have any comments then please send them to me at One Way UK's office.

Yours in His service

Peter Hellyer
Author   October 2002

Contents

Basic Tips On Puppetry
Harry Barrett

In Colossians 3: 23-24 we are all told *"Whatever you do, work at it with all your heart as working for the Lord, and not for men, since you know that you will receive an inheritance from the Lord as a reward."*

Learning correct puppetry techniques from the beginning is so important to the future development of your ministry.

Training the Leader / Director
To enable you to train your puppeteers successfully you first need to be trained. This training can come from attending one of our Puppet Ministry Training Events. In addition to this I would strongly recommend to you the **Reach for Heaven Puppet Ministry Training Video**, which covers not only basic training but also advanced puppetry. The video has the added benefit of enabling you to study in the comfort of your own home.

Training the Puppeteer
The length of time you spend training the puppeteer will depend largely on the number you are training and their ability to learn. I would normally work on a six to eight weeks training programme.

One of the most important things to remember is that **puppeteers need feedback**. After you have tought them the basics, it doesn't stop there. Training is an ongoing process and it is your responsibility to watch individual puppeteer's technique and give consistent and constructive feedback during the learning process. Never let puppeteers continue using incorrect or sloppy techniques.

Body Position
Standing or kneeling, are the two positions from which a puppeteer will normally operate a puppet. Don't allow your puppeteers to sit on chairs, as this will restrict not only their body movement but that of the puppet as well. When the puppeteer is in the kneeling position his or her body should be erect from the knees, with the arm extended straight up level with his or her ear. Never allow the puppeteer to bend their arm.

Entering and Exiting
When the puppet enters the stage it should look as if it is walking up stairs. To achieve this, the puppeteer should pivot his or her body away from the front of the stage so that the puppet has the depth. Now bring the puppet up as if it is walking up four steps.

Correct Height

When the puppet is on stage the audience should be able to see it from the belly button / waist up. If it is on stage with other puppets, then they all need to be the same height. This can be achieved by adjusting the height of the puppeteers with kneeling pads.

Good Eye Contact

This is important, your wrist needs to be cocked forward keeping the head of the puppet looking directly at the audience. This is so important if you are to communicate effectively to them.

Lip Synchronisation

Good lip synchronisation requires the puppet's mouth to be opened once for each syllable when singing or talking. **The "Puppet Aerobic" CD** is a great training tool and will help you immensely.

Mouth Action

Correct mouth action is a key part to being a good puppeteer. Practice opening the puppet's mouth **not** by moving your fingers upward **but by** dropping your thumb down. This is to make sure that the lower jaw of the puppet moves and not the top of the puppets head, which is referred to as "flipping the lid". This can be practiced in front of a mirror.

Posture

Good posture cannot be ignored. Your aim should be to have your puppet appear as natural as possible. To achieve this, the puppeteer's arm must be straight up, level with their ear (see illustration opposite). Do not allow your puppet to hang over the front of the stage or lean to the left or right.

Rod Arm Use

I would normally teach a new puppeteer Rod Arm technique in five to six weeks. The first thing a new puppeteer is taught about rods is how to put a rod onto a puppet.

The correct way to do this is very simple:

1.   Take your arm rod and a rubber band;

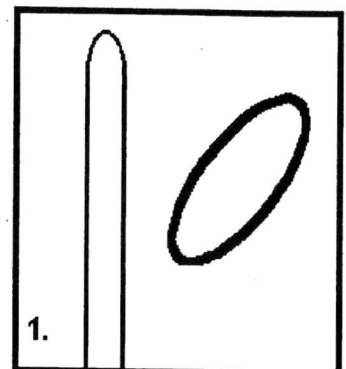

1.

2. tie the rubber band around the end of the rod by threading it through itself and pulling tight;

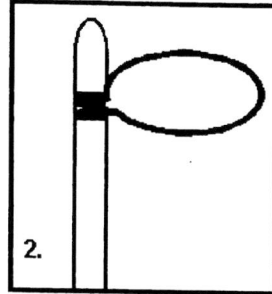

3. then make a "Bow and Arrow" shape with the rubber band and the rod;

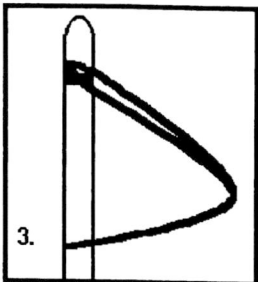

4. having done that, slip it over the puppet's arm, making sure that the rod is on the *inside* of the puppet's arm and the rubber band is facing outwards.

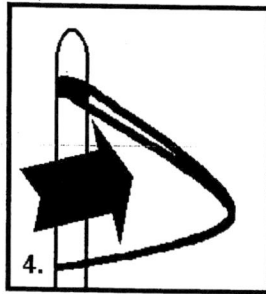

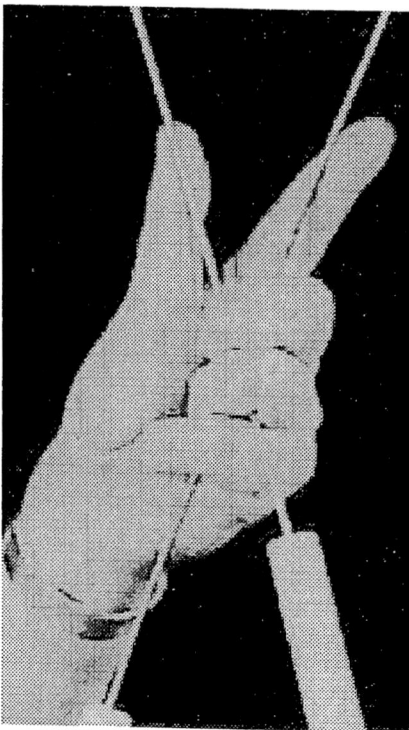

Once the arm rods are on both arms start practising with them. First use the left one then the right. As you get more confident in using them with your puppet practise some gestures, for example: blow a kiss, wave goodbye, brush your hair. Now start practising using both rods together. This is not as dificult as you may think.

First place the puppet on your hand and hold it strait up in the air. Now with your other hand and using your thumb, hook back the furthest rod (crossing over the other rod), capturing the other rod between your little finger. This is a bit like using chop sticks. Now practise making the puppet clap, cross it's arms, pray, look upset, and look happy.

I recommend you practise in front of a mirror or video yourself. Remember, whatever you do, work at it with all your heart as if working for the Lord.

8

Quick Index to subjects

Old Testament Events:
Six scripts on pages
10, 12, 14, 16, 18, 20.

Old Testament Heroines:
Five scripts on pages
22, 24, 26, 28, 30.

Old Testament Prophets:
Five scripts on pages
32, 34, 36, 38, 40.

New Testament Events:
Fourteen scripts on pages
42, 44, 46, 48, 50, 52, 54, 56, 58, 60, 62, 64, 66, 68.

New Testament Parables:
Nine scripts on pages
70, 72, 74, 76, 78, 80, 82, 84, 86.

Strictly for Camels!:
Five scripts on pages
88, 90, 92, 94, 96.

Conversations with Rockin' Rabbit:
Six scripts on pages
98, 100, 102, 104, 106, 108.

The Ark Idea
(Based upon Genesis 6:5-21)

Characters: **Noah and Noah's wife**

Stage: **Single level**

Scene: **Noah's home**

It is breakfast time and Noah's wife greets Noah as he enters.

Wife: Good morning Noah! What time did you come to bed then?

Noah: I'm not sure but it was very late.

Wife: What kept you up this time?

Noah: The Lord was speaking to me.

Wife: Again! It's a good job that I'm not a jealous woman because you seem to spend more time talking to him than me!

Noah: We live in serious times my dear. There's so much evil in the world.

Wife: Well I'm sure the Lord God is big enough to sort it all out without your help.

Noah: Of course he is, but the odd thing is he does want my help.

Wife: What more can he ask of you? As it is you're out every weekend preaching, telling people how they should live and how wrong sin is.

Noah: He wants me to build him something.

Wife: Before or after you build my new outhouse?

Noah: From what the Lord has told me we won't be needing a new outhouse.

Wife: Why ever not?

Noah: Because he plans to destroy the earth and everybody and everything in it by a flood. He is doing it because nobody has listened to my preaching.

Wife: Goodness me! And what's to become of the children and us?

Noah: He wants me to build a large boat for us so that we can be safe and float on the floodwaters.

Wife: And how long will that take, to build this boat?

Noah: A very long time, he wants it to be 135 metres long, 22.5 metres wide and 13.5 metres high.

Wife: But that's huge, we won't need all that space!

Noah: Well, the Lord has a little job for us to do. He wants us to take animals on board. Lots actually, all different types.

10

Wife:	What types? Be specific!
Noah:	Well, er, um, what's your favourite animal?
Wife:	You well know I'm not keen on animals but my cat's all right.
Noah:	We'll have a couple of cats on board. Come to think of it there'll be a couple of lions, cheetahs, tigers, lynxes, leopards…
Wife:	But those aren't cats they're wild animals. The hired men kill lions and leopards if they see them near our flocks.
Noah:	They're sort of cats, just bigger that's all.
Wife:	What's going on Noah? You'd better tell me everything!
Noah:	Put simply we are to take with us a pair of every type of animal and bird in the world. We will take more of the domestic animals that we use for food and to sacrifice. Our task is to repopulate the world with people and animals and birds.
Wife:	I don't believe it!
Noah:	Well it's true.
Wife:	Do the boys know this?
Noah:	Not yet I plan to tell them this evening. In the meantime I better start making arrangements to get all the timber and pitch we'll need to build the boat.
Wife:	What will happen to our neighbours?
Noah:	They'll be all swept away and drowned!
Wife:	That's horrible!
Noah:	So is how they live their lives, the Lord hates to see their lying, cheating, murdering, fighting and all their perversions. That's not what we were created for and he wants to start again.
Wife:	But it seems so cruel.
Noah:	How would you feel if it were your children out there involved in all their filth?
Wife:	I wouldn't like that at all!
Noah:	Then just think about how much love the Lord has for us. He wants to save us from destruction and give us a new chance to build a better world!

The Staff of God

(Based upon Exodus 17:8-13)

Characters: **Moses, Joshua, Aaron and Hur**

Stage: **Single level**

Scene 1: **Moses' tent**   **Scene 2:**   **A hilltop**

Scene 1:   *Moses' tent*

Moses is in his tent alone and Joshua enters

Joshua: Moses I have bad news!

Moses: What is it my son?

Joshua: The Amalekite army is gathering for an attack.

Moses: How do you see the position?

Joshua: It's difficult. We have far too many people and livestock to run for it.

Moses: So we have no real options do we?

Joshua: Not really.

Moses: Ask Aaron and Hur to come here.

Joshua exits

Moses: *Looking upwards* Lord I need your wisdom! What shall we do?

Joshua enters with Aaron and Hur

Aaron: You wanted to see us brother?

Moses: Has Joshua told you about the Amalekite army?

Aaron: Yes, he has.

Hur: Have you thought of what to do Moses?

Moses: If you mean have I asked the Lord God, yes I have.

Joshua: And what did he say?

Moses: Firstly, Joshua, mobilise our forces to attack the Amalekites tomorrow. Secondly, Aaron and Hur, we shall go to the top of the hill near here. We shall get a good view of the battlefield from there.

Aaron: What is your plan?

Moses: I shall hold up the staff of God before the Lord and he will remember us in our time of need.

Joshua: May I tell the men that, it will be a great encouragement.

Moses: Of course you may. Our future does not lie in our strength but in the faithfulness and might of the Lord God!   *They all exit.*

Scene 2:   *A hilltop*

Hur:	You were right Moses, we can see everything from this hill!
Moses:	Let me lift up the staff of God. May he see it and know our trust is in him to bring us victory!

Moses lifts up the staff of God standing behind Hur and Aaron

Hur:	The Amalekites are fighting strongly.
Aaron:	But Joshua is a good commander. Can you see how he has got men attacking the flanks of the main Amalekite column?
Hur:	Yes but the Amalekites are looking very strong.
Aaron:	I see what you mean our attack on their left flank has been pushed right back. Moses! Have you seen this?

Moses lowers his staff and moves forward

Aaron:	Look at that! Our main force is being pushed back now!
Moses:	I better lift the staff again.

Moses lifts the staff

Hur:	That's amazing! Our force on their left flank has come back so strongly it nearly cut their army in two.

Moses begins to weaken and the staff drops down

Aaron:	What's going on? The Amalekites have started pushing back our attacks on both their flanks!

Moses picks up the staff again and holds it high

Hur:	No it's all right our main force is now pressing in hard…

Moses begins to weaken and the staff drops down

	Oh no! The Amalekites are pressing forward again really strongly.
Aaron:	Moses! The staff! Every time you lift it up our army starts to win but every time you drop it down the Amalekites get stronger!
Moses:	Well don't just stand there like a couple of dummies! Help me hold the staff up!

Hur and Aaron stand either side of Moses and hold up his arms as he holds the staff

Aaron:	God is answering your prayer Moses, we're winning again!
Moses:	Good but don't waste your breath, either of you, we could be here until sunset! The Lord is doing his part, Joshua and our army are doing theirs, the least we can do is stand firm and persevere until victory is won!

That'll Do Donkey!

(Based upon Numbers 22:21-35)

Characters: Balaam, two male servants one animal: Balaam's ass

1 off-stage voice of an angel.

Stage: Single level

Scene: A road in the country, the two servants are following Balaam riding on his ass, hanging back they only talk to each other.

1st Servant: Not a very good rider is he?

2nd Servant: Who, Balaam?

1st Servant: Yes. Just look at him.

2nd Servant: He looks all right to me.

1st Servant: You wait …

The donkey with Balaam on his back swerves to the side; he hits it with a stick

2nd Servant: Well I never! What made it bolt like that? He surely doesn't have to hit the poor creature that hard.

The donkey with Balaam on his back gets back on course

1st Servant: Rather the ass gets it in the neck than us! Still looks like things are back under control. Good job too. The road narrows between two walls up ahead and then it gets even narrower a little further on.

2nd Servant: What's that animal doing? It's hugging that wall as if something is blocking the road.

1st Servant: Balaam should get it into the middle of the road otherwise he could crush his foot against the wall!

Balaam: Aaaah!

Balaam beats the ass again

2nd Servant: Too late he's hit the wall! I'm going to speak to him about hitting that animal!

1st Servant: Take my advice and keep quiet he's in a very bad mood. And watch out, you better drop behind me, the road really narrows here.

The donkey collapses under Balaam and the 1st Servant stops dead and the 2nd Servant bumps into him. Balaam beats the ass again

Balaam: Take that and that and that, you stupid animal!

Ass: What have I done to deserve such a beating?

Balaam: You've made me look a fool! If I had a sword I would kill you!

2nd Servant: What's going on?

1st Servant: Balaam's talking to his ass!

2nd Servant: Come again!

1st Servant: He's talking to his ass …

2nd Servant: Right! Has he lost the plot or something?

Ass: But I'm your very own ass. Have I ever done anything like this before?

Balaam: Well, no you haven't.

Ass: Then look ahead and see what I see.

Balaam stares off-stage in the direction they had been travelling and covers his eyes

Angel: Why did you beat your donkey three times? If the donkey had not shied away from me on those three occasions I would have killed you and saved the donkey!

Balaam: Oh forgive me! I never saw you standing in the road blocking my way.

2nd Servant: What's happening now? Is he still talking to the ass?

1st Servant: It's difficult to see the light is so bright but I think he's talking into thin air!

2nd Servant: He must be barking, absolutely barking!

Balaam: *To the angel off-stage.* If you want me to go home I will return.

Angel: No! Carry on your way with these men but remember this, you may only say what I tell you to say. You must only speak God's words and not what comes from yourself.

2nd Servant: What's up now?

1st Servant: That bright light has faded and Balaam is getting back on his ass. Looks like business as usual! He's moving on.

2nd Servant: Well better get a move on. You never know he may have another funny turn. By the way did you hear that ass speak?

1st Servant: I'm not sure but somebody other than Balaam definitely said something just after he stopped hitting it.

2nd Servant: Perhaps we should keep our heads down about this, eh?

Saul's Sacrifice

(Based upon 1 Samuel 13)

Characters: King Saul, Jonathan and Samuel.

Stage: Single level

Scene 1: Saul's campaign tent   **Scene 2:** Saul's campaign tent

Scene 1 *Saul and Jonathan are waiting for Samuel*

Saul: Is Samuel here yet?

Jonathan: No not quite.

Saul: What do you mean, not quite? We've waited long enough! Jonathan bring the sacrificial offerings to me. I'll make the sacrifice to the Lord.

Jonathan: But Father you can't do that! You're not anointed to make sacrifices.

Saul: Jonathan, let me remind you that our chief spy has said that the enemy has 30,000 chariots. It's unbelievable! 30,000 chariots!

Jonathan: But it may not be as bad as that. The other spy said that he had actually counted them and that there were only 3,000 chariots.

Saul: Well now, I've been worrying for nothing then! Only 3,000 chariots! Jonathan, how many chariots have we got? Would you like to step outside and count them for me? Or have you committed the number to memory?

Jonathan: Er, yes. Actually we don't happen to have any chariots at the moment.

Saul: At the moment we have no chariots! Are we expecting any to be delivered within the next day or so?

Jonathan: Bit pointless really, because we don't have any horses to pull them!

Saul: I'm glad I never gave you an expensive education because it would have been wasted on you. The enemy has at least 6,000 horses…

Jonathan: …They've got 12,000 at minimum because they've got 6,000 horseman in addition to the chariots and too many foot soldiers to count.

Saul: Thank you for making my day! Jonathan get this into your thick skull, you and I are the only people in our army who have proper weapons. Now unless I'm missing something two swords and two spears don't carry the clout of 3,000 chariots, 6,000 horseman and countless thousands of foot soldiers!

Jonathan: But we have he Lord on our side.

Saul:	Have we? Samuel is not here to make the sacrifices to ask the lord for his help.
Jonathan:	He said he will come and he always keeps his word.
Saul:	It's too late I will do it, prophets have no sense of timing! I'm anointed to rule this country so I can do what I jolly well like.
Scene 2:	*Samuel confronts Saul*
Samuel:	What were you doing out there?
Saul:	Making the sacrifices that you should have been making days ago! Have you seen the size of the army we face?
Samuel:	Have you any idea of the character of the God whom we serve?
Saul:	Look, Samuel, a lot of my men were beginning to run away, everybody was get jittery, you weren't here to perform the sacrifice, what was I to do?
Samuel:	You could have tried obedience that's always a good option.
Saul:	What do you mean?
Samuel:	By making the sacrifice you disobeyed the command of your Lord God. Had you obeyed and waited for me, the Lord would have established your kingdom over Israel forever!
Saul:	Well you can make sacrifices for me now, you can square things up!
Samuel:	Saul, you really don't understand do you? God is not your servant you were his! However, your reign will end because the Lord has found a man after his own heart to rule over the people.
Saul:	But why?
Samuel:	Because it is better to obey God than offer up sacrifices. He wanted your obedience not your lip service. He wanted you to be patient and wait trusting in him.
Saul:	But the enemy is out there, thousands of them, waiting to destroy us.
Samuel:	No Saul, you're wrong! The real enemy of a man is a heart that disobeys God!

Don't Anger God

(Based upon Proverbs 6:16-19 and Ephesians 4:31)

Characters: 3 girls; 2 spies; 1 man; 1 flower; and 1 off-stage Narrator

Stage: Single level

Scene: Plain stage

Narrator: Seven ways to anger God, no. 1, haughty eyes.

Two girls enter and stand centre stage. A third girl walks past them dressed unfashionably and stands alone to one side.

1st Girl: Look at Deirdre!

2nd Girl: Doesn't she look a sight!

1st Girl: Well she can't be in our gang if she looks like that!

2nd Girl: Let's leave now before I throw up!

Two girls exit, the third exits crying silently

Narrator: Seven ways to anger God, no. 2, a lying tongue.

Two girls enter and stand centre stage

1st Girl: Have you heard about Deirdre? She's been kissing spotty Tom!

2nd Girl: I don't believe it! Not spotty Tom?

1st Girl: Well, I think so, but don't quote me.

2nd Girl: You mean it may not be true?

1st Girl: Well that's what the younger sister of my older sister's last boyfriend's best friend said, I think!

2nd Girl: Well it must be true then!

Two girls exit

Narrator: Seven ways to anger God, no. 3, hands that kill the innocent.

A flower grows up centre stage, it speaks then two gloved hands strangle it and it disappears. The appearance of the butterfly and bees can be optional.

Flower: What a beautiful day! Hello Mr. Butterfly! Good morning Mrs. Bee! Hello sun! Hello trees! *The hands strike!*

Narrator: Seven ways to anger God, no. 4, a heart that plots evil.

Two mysterious figures in dark glasses creep towards each other from either side of the stage

1st Spy: Have you got the explosives?

2nd Spy: Yes, in my back pocket!

1st Spy: Whatever you do don't sit down! Do you know where to put it?

2nd Spy: Yes. I slip past Miss Piggy's dressing room and fix it to the door with the green star next to hers.

1st Spy: Then you attach the detonator and as soon as the studio manager calls…

2nd Spy: Kaboom! It's goodbye Kermit! *Both exit.*

Narrator: Seven ways to anger God, no. 5, feet that race to do wrong.

A spy enters and stands centre stage. A second spy enters quickly, speaks, and then both rush off

2nd Spy: *To 1st Spy* Noddy's out of town, let's trash his car! *Both exit.*

Narrator: Seven ways to anger God, no. 6, a false witness who pours out lies.

A girl is being interviewed by a female plain-clothes police officer

Officer: So you have said that you saw Deirdre going into the sweet shop.

Girl: Yes, she looked very hungry!

Officer: Then you say that you saw her running from the shop with ten large bags of humbugs.

Girl: Yes and twenty bars of chocolate!

Officer: How did she carry the ten large bags of humbugs and the twenty chocolate bars?

Girl: In her hands! She's got big hands, very big hands, they're enormous!

Officer: I think we both better go and see the Superintendent. *Both exit.*

Narrator: Seven ways to anger God, no. 7, a person who sows discord among brothers.

A football captain enters centre stage and addresses an imaginary team

Footballer: Curly, you may look good but, as John said to me, if you let another goal in like the 10 last week he and Geoff will give you a good kicking. Ernie, Tom hates it when you shout, so shut up! *Footballer exits.*

Narrator: God's word says, "Get rid of all bitterness, rage, anger, harsh words, and slander, as well as all types of malicious behaviour. Instead, be kind to each other, tender hearted, forgiving one another, just as God through Christ has forgiven you."

Fiery Furnace

(Based upon Daniel 3)

Characters:	**King Nebuchadnezzar; 2 Advisors; 3 Hebrews; and**
	1 off-stage Narrator
Stage:	**Single level**
Scene 1:	**The court of King Nebuchadnezzar**
Scene 2:	**The court of King Nebuchadnezzar Scene 3: By a furnace**

Narrator: Many years ago their lived a ruler of a mighty empire. The king was known for his bad temper. Being a mighty king he would think of things to do with his wealth to show off his great power. One day he woke up with a really big idea.

Scene 1: *The King is in his court with his advisers*

King: Officials listen to me!

Advisors: Yes, King Nebuchadnezzar, we only have ears for you!

King: This morning I woke up with a really big idea! I will build a huge golden statue on a flat area of land where it will stick up, tall, so everybody can see it.

1st Advisor: Your majesty that's an interesting idea, what will the statue do?

King: Do! Do! The statue won't DO anything it will BE, rather like me.

2nd Advisor: Excellent One yours is indeed an interesting and big idea but what will be the point of the statue?

King: Point! Point! Must it have a point?

2nd Advisor: Well, pyramids have a point!

King: Very true!

1st Advisor: The point of the statue better be metaphorical rather then literal otherwise it will look like a garden gnome!

King: That also is true. Let it's point be as a meeting place for all the leaders of the nation so that they may bow down and worship it.

2nd Advisor: And what if any should refuse to bow down and worship your statue?

King: Is that a possibility?

1st Advisor: All things are possible mighty King!

King: In that case let such a person be thrown into a fiery furnace!

2nd Advisor: Would your Majesty consider Community Service as an option?

King: No, if I ordered that, people might think I was going soft!

The King and his Advisors exit

Narrator: Three men refused to bow down to the golden statue, their names were Shadrach, Meshach and Abednego. The three were Jews who had been captured in Jerusalem as young men. They were brought before Nebuchadnezzar.

Scene 2:   *The King enters his court with Shadrach, Meshach and Abednego*

King: Do you understand that if you do not bow down to my statue that you will be thrown into the fiery furnace to be burned alive?

Shadrach: Your Majesty, our Lord God can save us from the fiery furnace.

Meshach: Your Majesty, even if our Lord God should choose not to save us…

Abednego: Then Your Majesty must understand that we will never serve your gods or bow down to your golden statue.

Narrator: In a furious temper the king ordered the three to be thrown into the furnace.

Exit Shadrach, Meshach and Abednego, followed by the King

Scene 3:   *By a furnace*

The King is seen looking into the furnace

King: What's happening! I can see the three men walking around unharmed and there is a fourth man with them! Get them out and bring them to me!

The three men enter before the King attended by the two advisors

King: Your God has saved you and your faith in him has been fully justified. Officials step forward!

Advisors: Yes, your Majesty!

King: I decree that nobody shall speak a word against the God of Shadrach, Meshach and Abednego. I further decree that if anybody does speak a word against their God then he shall be cut in pieces and his house burnt to the ground!

1ˢᵗ Adviser: Would your Majesty consider Community Service as an option?

King: No, if I ordered that, people might think I was going soft!

Rahab

(Based upon Joshua 2 and Hebrews 11:31)

Characters: **2 Israeli spies; a soldier of Jericho; Rahab of Jericho and her mother**

Stage: **2 levels**

Scene: **Rahab's house the bottom level is the ground floor and the upper level is the roof**

Rahab and her mother are in the ground floor of the house

Mother: Rahab! There's a couple of strange looking men skulking around outside!

Rahab: Let me have a look! They look like foreigners don't they.

Mother: May be they're spies from the Israelites!

Rahab: Mother you do have a vivid imagination. They're probably traders new to the town.

Mother: Well what are they doing around here. No respectable trader would come to this end of town.

Rahab: Perhaps they're lost. I'll call them and find out.

Mother: You'll do no such thing, what will the neighbours think?

Rahab: What they always think mother! Now go into the back room and I'll speak to them.

Mother exits

Rahab: Hello! Are you lost?

1st Spy: Why, yes! We were looking for somewhere to stay the night.

Rahab: Well, you're a long way from the commercial quarter.

2nd Spy: Is there anywhere around here we can stay?

Rahab: You'd be welcome here but all I can offer is the roof.

1st Spy: It's a warm night that will be fine.

Rahab: Come in, let me get you some wine and bread, you must be hungry.

2nd Spy: Thank you.

Rahab: Where are you from?

1st Spy: Why do you want to know?

Rahab: I'm interested in people that's why. Why are you here?

1st Spy: Does it really matter to you that much?

Rahab: If I'm putting you up I should know for how long.

1ˢᵗ Spy:	Do you need to know this minute?
2ⁿᵈ Spy:	What's that noise outside?
Rahab:	*Looking out of the door.* It's an army patrol!
1ˢᵗ Spy:	Look we're feeling very tired, can we skip the food and drink and get straight up to bed? We don't want to be disturbed because we've got a long day tomorrow.
2ⁿᵈ Spy:	Yes, if anybody asks there's no reason why they should know we're here, naturally we will pay very well for the extra privacy.
Rahab:	You're Israelites aren't you?
1ˢᵗ Spy:	What makes you think that?
Rahab:	Because you always answer a question with a question! Follow me to the roof. There are bundles of flax up there which I can use to hide you.
2ⁿᵈ Spy:	Bless you, you're a good woman.
Rahab:	That's one thing I'm not! But hurry I can hear the patrol again.

Rahab leads the spies from the lower stage to the upper stage where they lie down out of view. Rahab returns to the lower level, there is knocking at the door.

Soldier:	Open up! Open up!
Rahab:	There's no need to shout, it wasn't locked!
Soldier:	Two Israelite spies have been seen entering your house. Bring them out now!
Rahab:	Two men were here earlier but they didn't say they were spies. They left the city just before the gates closed for the night. I don't know where they were going but if you hurry you may catch them.
Soldier:	Thank you for your help, good night!

Soldier exits and Rahab returns to the roof where the two spies reappear

Rahab:	The soldiers have gone for now. Look I know the Lord God has given you this land. Everybody in the city is terrified of what's going to happen when you attack. We've all heard of the wonderful things your God has done. I believe what God has planned will happen. Promise me that you will save my family and me because I've helped you.
1ˢᵗ Spy:	Don't betray us, hang a scarlet rope out of your window and we will make sure nobody in this house is harmed. You have shown favour to God's people, now our God will surely show favour to you!

Deborah

(Based upon Judges 4)

Characters:	**Barak and Deborah**
Stage:	**Single level**
Scene:	**Outdoors under the palm tree of Deborah.**

Deborah: Greetings, Barak! I am pleased to see you.

Barak: Greetings Judge Deborah! Why have you called for me?

Deborah: I have received a commandment from the Lord God to pass on to you.

Barak: Me?

Deborah: You are Barak, son of Abinoam?

Barak: Yes.

Deborah: You are Barak, son of Abinoam, who lives in Kedesh in the land of Naphtali?

Barak: Yes.

Deborah: Then the message I have would appear to be for you dear boy. It is comforting to know that the Lord God has not got it wrong!

Barak: I didn't mean to suggest...

Deborah: Good! Then don't! The Lord God has seen how we Israelites have been under the heel of King Jabin of Hazor and his army commander, Sisera for 20 years. This was because our people lived lives that were evil in the sight of the Lord God. However, the Lord has heard our prayers for help.

Barak: That's good news but what has it to do with me?

Deborah: Quite a lot evidently because the Lord commands you to raise an army of 10,000 warriors.

Barak: But how can I do that?

Deborah: You will recruit them from the tribes of Naphtali and Zebulun. They know you there.

Barak: But what do I know of military strategy?

Deborah: The Lord says that he will lure Sisera and his army to the Kishon River and that is where he will give you victory over them.

Barak: I don't know.

Deborah: What is there to know? The Lord is on your side; he will give you victory! What is there to discuss? Obey the Lord and you will succeed.

Barak:	I will go, but only if you go with me!
Deborah:	I beg your pardon? I'm a judge and a prophet not a mascot!
Barak:	I mean it! I will do as the Lord asks but only if you go with me!
Deborah:	Well all right but why?
Barak:	Sisera has vastly superior forces. He has 900 iron chariots besides his foot soldiers.
Deborah:	And do you think I will frighten them, I am not sure whether to be flattered or insulted! Don't you think the Lord is well able to deal with Sisera's chariots?
Barak:	What do you mean?
Deborah:	What is the land like around the Kishon river?
Barak:	Flat, good chariot country.
Deborah:	Except in the wet! Sisera's chariots will get bogged down in the wet, just like the wheels came off the chariots of Pharaoh's army when they chased Moses.
Barak:	How do you know all this?
Deborah:	Because I listen to the Lord God. If you listened to him rather than your fears the glory of victory would go to you. As it is you will receive no honour and Sisera will be destroyed by a woman!

Ruth

(Based upon the book of Ruth)

Characters:	**Naomi; Ruth and off-stage Narrator**
Stage:	**Single level**
Scene 1:	**Naomi's home in Moab Scene 2: Naomi's home in Bethlehem**
Scene 1:	*Naomi's home in Moab*

Narrator: In the land of Moab there lived a widow. Shortly after her husband died she lost both her sons too. One of her daughter in laws decided to stay in Moab but the other had different ideas!

Naomi: Ruth you are a good girl and I love you. Now my husband is dead and my sons are dead I have decided to return to my own country. You my dear should remain in your own country.

Ruth: But I don't wish to stay here. I will go where you go. I will live where you live. Your people will be my people. Your God will be my God.

Naomi: Is there nothing I can say to persuade you to stay?

Ruth: Nothing, I shall go with you to your hometown.

Naomi: Bethlehem is a long way away.

Ruth: Then the sooner we start the better!

Both exit

Scene 2: *Naomi's home in Bethlehem*

There is a knock on the door and Ruth enters

Naomi: Ruth, where have you been?

Ruth: I've been to get some food for us.

Naomi: I hope you were careful!

Ruth: I've returned safely haven't I? I trusted the Lord God to guide me. He looked after me, and he will continue to look after us.

Naomi: Where did you glean all the corn?

Ruth: I gleaned the corn in the fields of a man called Boaz.

Naomi: Boaz!

Ruth: Yes, he was very kind to me.

Naomi: You spoke to him?

Ruth: Yes. He told me exactly where I could glean his fields safely. I think he told his workers to drop extra corn where I was gleaning. There was

	more than I could carry.
Naomi:	That's because he knows about you.
Ruth:	How does he know about me?
Naomi:	He's a relative of mine. He will have heard of what you said to me when we were in Moab.
Ruth:	What was that?
Naomi:	You remember, "I will go where you go. I will live where you live. Your people will be my people. Your God will be my God." Do you realise that as a relative he has a right to marry you?
Ruth:	He wouldn't want to marry me!
Naomi:	Why not? You are loving, hardworking and beautiful! In whichever order you place them those are three very good reasons why Boaz should want to marry you.
Ruth:	He was very kind to me and he treated his workers with respect, not many men do that. It would be wonderful if he wanted to marry me.
Naomi:	I'm sure that he will do everything he can to do so! In the meantime let me tell you what you can do.

Both exit

| **Narrator:** | The day came when Naomi had something special to say to Ruth. |

Ruth and Naomi enter

Ruth:	What did you want to say to me Naomi?
Naomi:	I've had a visit from Boaz. He had something to ask me.
Ruth:	What was that?
Naomi:	He asked me if you would be his wife.
Ruth:	He asked you if I would be his wife!
Naomi:	I told him that I thought you would!
Ruth:	The Lord God has really blessed me!
Naomi:	He's blessed you because you blessed me first. You refused to let me come home alone and you have worked hard to keep us both. Just as you've cared for me the Lord has cared for you!
Narrator:	The Lord God blessed Ruth with a son called Obed, he had a son called Jesse and he had a son called David who became Israel's most famous king. And it all happened because Ruth said to Naomi "I will go where you go. I will live where you live. Your people will be my people. Your God will be my God." And, of course because Ruth said "Yes!" to Boaz.

Hannah

(Based upon 1 Samuel 1- 2:11)

Characters: **Elkanah, Eli, Peninnah and Hannah**

Stage: **Single level**

Scene 1: **Elkanah's home**   **Scene 2:** **The Tabernacle**

Scene 3: **Elkanah's home**

Scene 1: *Peninnah and Hannah are talking together*

Peninnah: Hannah I cannot understand why Elkanah continues to love you.

Hannah: Why shouldn't he love me?

Peninnah: Do men love dry unproductive gardens? Do men love dry riverbeds? Let's face it dear you are as dry as they are!

Hannah: You're so cruel! I would love to bear children for Elkanah!

Peninnah: You mustn't let it worry you my dear. After all he still loves you, though God alone knows why! And as for children, I can bear sufficient for both of us, you can be sure of that!

Hannah starts to sob silently as Peninnah exits and Elkanah enters

Elkanah: Why Hannah, you are crying? Come, come, what's upset you?

Hannah: Elkanah, I so want to give you a child.

Elkanah: But Hannah, is that so important? I love you so much, aren't I better than 10 sons to you?

Hannah: But Peninnah says…

Elkanah: Peninnah says lots of things that would be better unsaid. Come we must start our journey to Shiloh to visit the Tabernacle of the Lord.

Hannah and Elkanah exit

Scene 2: *Hannah and Elkanah are in the Tabernacle*

Elkanah: Hannah are you coming back to our tent?

Hannah: Not for a while, I want to continue praying.

Elkanah: Do you want me to stay?

Hannah: No, please go back and join the others, I'll be all right.

Elkanah exits and Hannah begins to pray silently, her mouth moves but she is silent

Hannah: Lord Almighty, please see my sorrow and answer my prayer! Lord please give me a son, then I promise I will give him back to you. He will be yours for his entire lifetime, dedicated to you.

Hannah begins to cry quietly then prays in silence but her mouth is moving. As

Eli enters and sees Hannah praying, he thinks she is drunk

Eli: *Talking to himself.* What on earth is that woman doing? It looks as if she's drunk!

Eli moves across to Hannah

Eli: Must you come into the Tabernacle of God drunk!

Hannah: Oh no Sir! I'm not drunk, just very sad and I was pouring out my grief to the Lord.

Eli: I am sorry to have misjudged you. Whatever your request may the Lord give it to you, go and rejoice that you have God's favour!

Hannah: Thank you! Thank you! I will rejoice that God has heard my prayer!

Hannah and Eli exit

Scene 3:   *Elkanah and Hannah enter their home arm in arm*

Elkanah: What has happened to you Hannah? Ever since we returned from Shiloh you've been so different! There's been no more not eating, I don't find you crying and whatever Peninnah says never seems to upset you now.

Hannah: Can't you guess?

Elkanah: Guess what?

Hannah: Elkanah, the Lord God has answered my prayer!

Elkanah: What prayer?

Hannah: Don't you know anything?

Elkanah: Well I'm not a woman so I'm not a mind reader!

Hannah: Dear Elkanah, I asked the Lord for a son and I'm going to have a baby!

Elkanah: Oh my! Quick you'd better sit down!

Hannah: *Laughing* I'm not sick, I'm pregnant!

Elkanah: Well in that case I'd better sit down!

Hannah: Now listen! When my baby boy is weaned we shall go together to the Tabernacle at Shilo. Then I shall put him into the care of Eli, the High Priest. That is what I promised the Lord. Our son will become a great man of God.

Elkanah: But you have waited so long for a child how could you do that?

Hannah: I promised the Lord I would. He kept his side of the agreement so I must keep mine. I know I shall bear other children have no fear!

Elkanah: What shall we call our son?

Hannah: Samuel it means "heard of God" and God said "yes" to my prayer!

The Widow's Jar

(Based upon: 2 Kings 4:1-7 and Matthew 6:8)

Characters: **Elisha and a poor widow**

Stage: **Single level**

Scene 1: **Elisha's home** **Scene 2:** **Elisha's home**

Scene 1: *Elisha is in his home when he hears a knock at the door*

Elisha: Hello! Who's there? Come in!

Widow: *Entering the room.* It's me. Do you remember, before he died my husband served you faithfully?

Elisha: I do indeed. He was a good man who feared the Lord. What did you want to see me about?

Widow: I'm in terrible trouble.

Elisha: What's happened?

Widow: I owe some money that I cannot pay back. I had to borrow the money to keep my two boys and myself alive. But now the person who lent me the money has threatened to take my two sons as slaves if I don't pay him!

Elisha: I see, things are serious! Tell me, what have you got at home?

Widow: Nothing, nothing at all!

Elisha: Just think carefully. Don't rush just be calm.

Widow: Calm! That's easy to say!

Elisha: It just occurred to me that you may have something at home so common place you might have overlooked it.

Widow: No I've nothing except a jar of olive oil.

Elisha: Ah! Just as I thought! Now listen carefully and I will tell you what to do. First of all borrow as many jars and containers as you can from your neighbours.

Widow: How am I going to carry them all? My neighbours live this way and that; it'll mean a lot of walking.

Elisha: If I were you I would use those two sons of yours. I'm sure they will be very good at fetching and carrying, especially because it will save them from slavery! When you've got all the jars and containers you can find go into your house with your sons and shut the door.

Widow: What do I do then?

Elisha:	Pour olive oil from your jar into all the other jars…
Widow:	But…
Elisha:	No "Buts", just do it!
Scene 2:	*Elisha enters his home with the widow*
Elisha:	It's good to see you again. How have things gone?
Widow:	Very well. I did just as you told me. I sent my boys out to my neighbours. They went this way and that, all over the place.
Elisha:	So they found a good number of jars and containers?
Widow:	I should think so! They covered my table, they were stacked all over the floor.
Elisha:	Then what happened?
Widow:	I did exactly as you told me. I and my boys closed the door and began to pour the oil from my jar. Every single jar and container was filled. My jar kept pouring until when I asked for another jar from one of my sons he told me that not a single empty jar was left. At that moment the oil stopped flowing from my jar!
Elisha:	And?
Widow:	Well, what do I do now?
Elisha:	Go and sell all the oil you have. You'll find that you will have enough money to pay your debts.
Widow:	Oh thank you!
Elisha:	That's not all! When you have paid your debts you'll find that you will have plenty of money for you and your sons to live off!
Widow:	I don't know what to say!
Elisha:	If I were you I would praise the Lord for his goodness to you. Always remember that he cares for you and knows exactly what you need even before you ask him!

Eijah Hides

(Based upon 1 Kings 19:8-18)

Characters: **Elijah and the off-stage voice of God**

Stage: **Single level**

Scene: **In a cave on Mount Sinai**

God:	Good morning Elijah!
Elijah:	Oh Lord, it's you!
God:	Yes, it is I! Elijah what are you doing hiding in this cave?
Elijah:	Your angel came and told me to come to Mount Sinai Lord.
God:	Where did my angel find you?
Elijah:	Hiding in the desert Lord.
God:	And why were you hiding in the desert, Elijah?
Elijah:	Jezebel, wife of King Ahab of Israel wants to kill me!
God:	Does that come as a surprise to you?
Elijah:	What do you mean Lord?
God:	Elijah, I seem to remember that you killed 450 prophets of Baal in the Kishon Valley. You know that Jezebel loves her false religion. I observed that she was just a teensy bit annoyed by this set back.
Elijah:	She made me afraid.
God:	Ah, yes! The scary woman syndrome!
Elijah:	Lord, I sense that I have done something wrong.
God:	I wouldn't put it like that Elijah but I do have a question to ask you.
Elijah:	What is that Lord?
God:	Who helped you overcome the prophets of Baal?
Elijah:	You did Lord! I couldn't have done anything without you!
God:	Does it not occur to you Elijah that I who helped you against 450 raving, knife wielding prophets might have been able to afford you some little assistance against one, albeit scary, woman?
Elijah:	Yes Lord but all of your prophets have been killed, I'm the only one left who worships you. The people of Israel have torn down your altars and broken their covenant with you.
God:	Things are not quite as they seem, Elijah. I want you to go back the way you came here. I have work for you to do and the scary woman won't interfere.

Elijah:	But Lord…
God:	Now I don't want any more buts, Elijah.
Elijah:	No Lord.
God:	Go to the wilderness of Damascus and anoint Hazael to be king of Aram.
Elijah:	Yes Lord.
God:	Then anoint Jehu son of Nimshi to be king of Israel. Be careful if you see him in a chariot, he drives like a maniac!
Elijah:	Yes Lord, so I've heard!
God:	It's close to the time when you must come home so find Elisha son of Shaphat and anoint him to replace you as my prophet. Have you got all that, Elijah?
Elijah:	Yes Lord.
God:	And Elijah, you're not alone, there are many people in Israel who have stayed faithful to me and have never worshipped Baal.
Elijah:	There are Lord?
God:	Yes, quite a lot, actually.
Elijah:	But I've never seen them!
God:	Some of them may never have seen you but it doesn't mean you don't exist!
Elijah:	No I suppose not Lord.
God:	Would you believe that there are 7,000, Elijah?
Elijah:	No Lord, I wouldn't!
God:	I thought you'd say that but you're wrong. There are 7,000 who have remained faithful to me.
Elijah:	That's amazing Lord!
God:	What is it about you prophets that makes you think that you're the only one's around who care about me. I tell you Elijah my people are in the most surprising places. When you come and join me you'll find out. I hope that you're not disappointed that you weren't the only one?
Elijah:	No Lord. It's good to know that I'm not alone, even if I can't see them.
God:	None of my people are ever alone. I have my witnesses everywhere!

Elijah and Ahab

(Based upon 1 Kings 21:1-21)

Characters: **Elijah and the off-stage voice of God**

Stage: **Single level**

Scene: **In Elijah's home**

God: Elijah!

Elijah: Yes Lord! I'm listening.

God: King Ahab has been sulking again!

Elijah: What is it about this time Lord?

God: He wanted to buy Naboth's vineyard, the one that is by his palace.

Elijah: I doubt whether Naboth would sell that, it's been in his family for years.

God: That's why Ahab was sulking, Naboth wouldn't sell!

Elijah: Forgive me Lord but what has this to do with me?

God: I want you to give to give a message to Ahab from me.

Elijah: You mean the "Why don't you ask me if you wanted a vineyard?" type message?

God: No Elijah it's too late for that type of message.

Elijah: Why?

God: Because Ahab's wife Jezebel arranged for Naboth to be killed so that the king could have his vineyard.

Elijah: That's terrible, Naboth was a good man.

God: Envy is a great evil and envy for Naboth's vineyard had gripped Ahab's heart. He could get no rest thinking about it, so Jezebel decided to act.

Elijah: But what message do you want me to give to Ahab?

God: You will find him in Naboth's vineyard, taking possession of his ill-gotten gains!

Elijah: Will Jezebel be there?

God: Ah, yes, you're not keen on her are you?

Elijah: Well Lord, she's one scary woman!

God: Don't worry Elijah, my message will make you one scary prophet! In any event Jezebel will not be there.

Elijah: But the message Lord? What do I say to Ahab?

God: Ask him on my behalf "Isn't killing Naboth bad enough? Must you also steal from him." Tell him that because he has done this the dogs will lick up his blood outside the city. Yes, they will lick up his blood in the same way they licked up the blood of poor Naboth after they had stoned him to death.

Elijah: Phew! Lord that's a heavy-duty prophecy to give!

God: Sin is heavy-duty, Elijah!

Elijah: Yes Lord!

God: But there's more Elijah.

Elijah: I thought there might be. It's Jezebel isn't it?

God: Yes and all Ahab's family. I want you to tell him that all his family will be destroyed, totally.

Elijah: Does that include Jezebel too?

God: Yes but there is some detail I would like to add in her case.

Elijah: Dogs, Lord?

God: Yes Elijah, dogs. Tell Ahab that the dogs will eat her body by the city wall. Come to think of it you may as well tell him that the dogs will eat all his family members who die in the city.

Elijah: That's gross!

God: Not as gross as the sins of Ahab and Jezebel! Elijah this is serious you seem not to have got the point.

Elijah: I'm sorry Lord.

God: I think even your senses are becoming dulled by the sin around you. Ahab has been more sold out to doing what I consider to be evil than anybody else I can think of. As for Jezebel she encouraged him in his sin every step of the way.

Elijah: But what if Ahab repented, in spite of being so wicked in your sight?

God: He will, Elijah, he will! He will tear his clothes, dress himself in sackcloth and fast. Ahab will listen to you and I will forgive him.

Elijah: But why Lord, when he has been so evil?

God: Because Elijah, for all his evil I love Ahab. In fact I won't reject anybody who comes to me sorry for the bad, vile or disgusting things they've done. I love people, Elijah and I want to see them living well.

Isaiah

(Based upon Isaiah 20)

Characters:	**Isaiah and the off-stage voice of God**
Stage:	**Single level**
Scene:	**Isaiah's home**

God: Isaiah, I have a special task for you!

Isaiah: Yes Lord what is it?

God: I want to prophesy in a very special way to the nations of Egypt and Ethiopia.

Isaiah: And what do you want to say to them?

God: Nothing yet, I want to wait for three years before actually giving the message.

Isaiah: I see Lord so you want me to prepare them for the message?

God: Well put Isaiah that's exactly it!

Isaiah: So how do you want me to prepare them for the message?

God: I would like you to give them a special sign.

Isaiah: Which will last for three years?

God: Yes, a special sign that will last for three years.

Isaiah: And what sign do you want me to give them Lord?

God: Ah, yes! The sign I want you to give them.

Isaiah: Yes Lord, the sign what is it?

God: I would like you to take all your clothes and your shoes off and walk around naked for three years.

Isaiah: Lord is that you speaking to me?

God: You know my voice Isaiah.

Isaiah: Yes Lord, I do. May I just repeat your message to see that I have understood it correctly?

God: Please do.

Isaiah: You would like me to take all my clothes and my shoes off and walk around naked for three years?

God: Perfect, you've repeated the message perfectly.

Isaiah: And you want me to walk naked…

God: All the year around, winter and summer etc, etc.

Isaiah: Yes Lord. May I ask what will happen after three years.

God:	After three years I will say that you have been walking around naked and barefoot for three years as a sign, a symbol, of the troubles which will come upon Egypt and Ethiopia.
Isaiah:	What troubles Lord?
God:	The king of Assyria will attack them and take away the Egyptians and Ethiopians as captives. When he does he will force them to walk naked and barefoot so that they will be ashamed.
Isaiah:	I understand how they'll feel.
God:	You don't yet Isaiah but you will after three years of …
Isaiah:	Walking around naked.
God:	You know how reliant the Philistines have become upon the power of Ethiopia and their treaties with Egypt. They will be staggered when they see what happens because they will realise if such a terrible thing can happen to their allies what hope do they have?
Isaiah:	That's a stark message Lord!
God:	And it demands a stark sign to prepare them for it!
Isaiah:	Yes Lord, I see that.
God:	But do you understand Isaiah that I want people to understand that I love them and I don't want to see them go to disaster?
Isaiah:	I think so Lord.
God:	Isaiah, I know this is a difficult task but I will go to any lengths to save people from their sin.
Isaiah:	Any lengths Lord?
God:	Any lengths, Isaiah. One day I will tell you of the plan I have in place to… No the time is not yet, but I will tell you. In the meantime…
Isaiah:	It's off with the clothes and …
God:	Out into the street for …
Isaiah:	Three years! I hope the people are ready for this!

Jeremiah

(Based upon Jeremiah 13:1-11)

Characters: **Jeremiah and the off-stage voice of God**

Stage: **Single level**

Scene: **In Jeremiah's home**

God:	Jeremiah!
Jeremiah:	Yes Lord!
God:	I'd like you to go and buy a new belt.
Jeremiah:	Yes, Lord. Any particular type of belt?
God:	I would like you to buy a linen belt.
Jeremiah:	Yes Lord, a linen belt.
God:	And Jeremiah, make sure that you don't wash the belt when you've bought it.
Jeremiah:	But Lord, everybody knows that you must wash linen belts when you buy them because it makes them stronger.
God:	Not this one you don't because…
Jeremiah:	Because you don't want me to Lord.
God:	That's right, Jeremiah, because I don't want you to wash this belt.
Jeremiah:	So shall I wear the belt when I have bought it Lord?
God:	Of course, why else should you buy a linen belt if not to wear it?
Jeremiah:	Even though I won't…
God:	…Wash it to make it stronger! That's right Jeremiah.
Jeremiah:	Lord, is there a special reason for wearing the belt.
God:	Yes.
Jeremiah:	May I know what the reason is?
God:	Yes.
Jeremiah:	What is the reason?
God:	In a little while I will ask you to take it off.
Jeremiah:	Right! I buy a new linen belt, do not wash it to make it strong and…
God:	In a little while I will ask you to take it off. That's right Jeremiah.
Jeremiah:	When I come to take the belt off, am I to do something with it?
God:	Oh yes! You are to put it somewhere special.
Jeremiah:	And where shall that be Lord?
God:	I will ask you to go down to the River Euphrates.

Jeremiah:	But you can't hide a belt in the river, it will float away!
God:	I know Jeremiah, I know! May I finish what I was going to say?
Jeremiah:	I'm sorry Lord, please continue.
God:	Once you are by the river I shall ask you to look for a hole in the rocks by the riverbank. You can put the new linen belt in the hole.
Jeremiah:	But Lord, if I do that and leave it there, the river's water will weaken and rot the linen.
God:	Yes, Jeremiah, that occurred to me too. But I shan't forget the belt. I shall let it remain hidden for some time but then I shall ask you to go and find it again.
Jeremiah:	But when I do find it, the belt will be…
God:	Completely useless! Yes, Jeremiah, I know but I shall still ask you to take it home.
Jeremiah:	Lord, is there a purpose to doing that?
God:	Jeremiah, have you ever known me do anything without having a good reason?
Jeremiah:	No Lord, I haven't.
God:	When you find the linen belt again you'd better be careful with it because it will tear easily. However, as I have said I would like you to take it home.
Jeremiah:	And when I've taken it home Lord, what then?
God:	I'm glad you asked me that, Jeremiah. When you have the belt at home, look at it carefully. You see that belt represents my people.
Jeremiah:	Your people, Lord?
God:	Yes! My people have been created to remain really close to me, just like a belt fixed around somebody's waist. But instead of listening to me and doing what pleases me, my people often decide to please themselves. They ignore me and all the good things I have planned for them. They go off and do what they want to do instead. Anybody who turns his or her back on me is like a linen belt that becomes rotten and useless because it has not been cared for properly!
Jeremiah:	Lord, I never want to become like that!
God:	Then obey my commandments and you never shall!

Ezekiel

(Based upon Ezekiel 4)

Characters: **Ezekiel and the off-stage voice of God**

Stage: **Single level**

Scene: **Ezekiel's home**

God: Ezekiel, I want you to warn the people of Jerusalem about what will happen to them because they have turned their backs on me!

Ezekiel: Yes Lord, what do you want me to do?

God: I want you to act out the disaster that will come upon them.

Ezekiel: How shall I do that?

God: Get a large brick or tile. I would like you take it outside into the street so that everybody can see what you are doing with it.

Ezekiel: Certainly Lord that shouldn't be too difficult! What next?

God: Scratch a map of Jerusalem onto it and build up model siege ramps against the city walls.

Ezekiel: I've got that Lord. Then what?

God: Take one of those iron griddles from your kitchen and put it between you and the model city, demonstrating how the enemy will attack Jerusalem. All of this will be a warning to the people.

Ezekiel: Right! I'd better go off and…

God: Wait a moment Ezekiel, I've not finished yet!

Ezekiel: I'm sorry Lord, what else is there?

God: I want you to lie on your left side and carry the sins of Israel for how long you lie there.

Ezekiel: Yes Lord, how long do I do that for, a couple of hours?

God: I was thinking of something longer.

Ezekiel: You mean like day?

God: Certainly days come into it.

Ezekiel: Days?

God: Yes, 390 of them to be precise. You see that's a good number because it's one day for every year of Israel's sin. But you get to move after 390 days.

Ezekiel: I do?

God:	Yes because you'll roll over onto your right side and carry the sins of Judah for another 40 days, one day for...
Ezekiel:	Each year of Judah's sin. I understand Lord.
God:	Good, I knew I could rely on you Ezekiel. Of course you will carry on with your demonstration of the siege of Jerusalem.
Ezekiel:	Naturally, I had assumed that of course.
God:	Just so you don't wriggle about and distract people from getting the point I shall see to it that you are tied up so that you cannot move from side to side.
Ezekiel:	Yes, most helpful!
God:	Get some grain and beans together and make bread in front of the people. Of course you must ration it out carefully, just about 228 grams a day will do, prepare it as you would barley cakes. Oh yes, and allow yourself a little over half a litre of water a day too.
Ezekiel:	What shall I use to cook with?
God:	Use human dung, dried of course, I really want them to get the point.
Ezekiel:	No Lord, I'm sorry but that's enough! The toy city, the 390 days, the 40 days, the ropes, the ridicule, I can take all that for you Lord but cooking on human dung…it's disgusting…I've never done anything dirty like that in my life before, please don't ask me to do it now!
God:	Ok Ezekiel, I hear what you're saying. Just for you, forget the human dung you can use cow dung instead.
Ezekiel:	That's a concession!
God:	Ezekiel, this exhibition is not being performed for your benefit!
Ezekiel:	I'd gathered that!
God:	I want the people to understand the seriousness of their sin and the terrible consequences that it will have upon their lives.
Ezekiel:	Yes Lord, I'm sorry but it's just that...
God:	I know, you've never done anything dirty and you don't want to start now but Ezekiel catch sight of what I'm doing. You will be showing them what will happen if they carry on living as they are. I must warn them, I love them too much not to warn them. I just want them to return to me.

Squeeze Up!

(Based upon Luke 2:5-7)

Characters: **A donkey, cow and sheep and an off-stage male voice**

Stage: **Single level**

Scene: **A stable**

Donkey and cow are standing together

Donkey:	Where's Sheep gone?
Cow:	She's gone outside to look around.
Donkey:	What for? There's no occasion to go looking around at this time of night. She'll only disturb us when she comes back and lets in all the cold air!
Cow:	She wanted to find out what all the noise is about.
Donkey:	Well I could have told her that! It's people, they always make noise!
Cow:	What do you mean?
Donkey:	First thing they do when they open the door in the morning is shout "Gerrup!" Then they stick my harness on and it's "Gerrout!" Then they pile packs on my back and it's "Gerron!" Do they think I'm stupid or something?
Cow:	But this is not everyday work noise, it's different.
Donkey:	Oh yes, like it is!
Cow:	There's a constant hum like bees around bougainvillaea. There's the tramp of feet like they were treading grapes. There's a thrill of expectancy in the air like the first balmy breezes of spring.
Donkey:	You get quite poetical for a bovine at times! Look it's people and people make noise, it goes with the territory. They are noisy, they've always been noisy and they will continue to be noisy!
Cow:	No this is different. Yesterday when I was out I saw lots of people I've never seen before.
Donkey:	Like you move in high society!
Cow:	The square was full camels and donkeys and they were all strangers. Didn't you notice something different?
Donkey:	With the weights I have to carry I never lift my eyes off the road for a second. I can't afford the luxury of staring around when I'm working.
Cow:	Listen I think Sheep is coming back.

Donkey: More likely people. If it's noise you can hear it'll be people!

The sheep enters the stable

Cow: Hello Sheep! What's happening?

Sheep: Plenty! Something special must be going to happen. The place is crawling with people and strange camels and donkeys.

Donkey: I told you it would be people didn't I? It's nothing to do with us so we can get to sleep.

Sheep: I don't think we'll get much sleep tonight.

Donkey: Why is that?

Sheep: Because some people will be staying here tonight!

Cow: How exciting!

Donkey: How do you know?

Sheep: The innkeeper's dog told me.

Donkey: You don't want to believe what old flea bait tells you. He's about as reliable as a leaky bucket!

Sheep: No it's true. There are so many people in town that every spare bit of space is being used. Something very important must being going to happen. There isn't even any room left in the inn!

Donkey: Well there's no point in you settling down now.

Sheep: Why not?

Donkey: If you're right and people are going to sleep in this stable we'll get the old "Gerrup! Gerrout!" treatment, mark my words!

Cow: Don't listen to him, there'll be plenty of room if we all squeeze up a bit!

Donkey: You just don't get it do you? People don't squeeze up a bit they take over!

Sheep: I think I hear the innkeeper's footsteps now!

Voice: Gerrup! Gerrout! I've got to clean this place up for guests.

Donkey: What did I say? If anything important does happen tonight they'll remember all about there being no room left in the inn but I bet they'll forget about there being no room in the stable for us!

To Touch Him

(Based upon: Matthew 9:20, Mark 5:25; Luke 8:43-48)

Characters: Jesus & 2 disciples. 2 women + other puppets as crowd

Stage: Single level

Scene: **A street with a crowd waiting for Jesus; two women are standing centre stage in front of the crowd.**

1st Woman: Are you sure you want to do this?

2nd Woman: I must. If I can just get to touch him, I'll be healed!

1st Woman: Well, don't get your hopes up.

2nd Woman: What do you mean, I've tried every doctor around and they couldn't do anything for me!

1st Woman: That's my point. If they couldn't help you what makes you think this man can?

2nd Woman: Haven't you heard the stories?

1st Woman: We've all heard the stories dear. But who knows the truth?
Some of it could be just to get a good crowd along to his meetings!

2nd Woman: How can you say that? He's healed real people with real problems. There are names, places, dates and times. We're not talking fiction! This man heals and if he can heal others he can heal me!

1st Woman: Well, you're persistent, I'll give you that.

2nd Woman: Meaning don't be disappointed if he doesn't heal you?

1st Woman: You want to watch out for the "This friend told me about his friend who had a friend who knew someone who saw somebody being healed..." stuff!

1st Woman: Don't you want to see me made well?

2nd Woman: Of course I do but I don't want to see you disappointed either.

1st Woman: Looks like we'll both find out the truth soon. I think I can see him.

2nd Woman: Where? Which one's him?

1st Woman: The one in the middle.

2nd Woman: How do you know? Have you seen him before?

1st Woman: No, but I'm sure it is.

Jesus enters between two disciples; as He passes the 2nd Woman she bends down to touch Him and the crowd pushes around Him. Jesus and His disciples stop.

Jesus:	Who touched me?
Disciple:	Lord, are you joking? Look at the crowd, everybody's touching us!
Jesus:	No, somebody touched me deliberately. I felt the power go out of me. Who touched me?
2nd Woman:	Lord, it was me! I touched you.
Jesus:	Daughter why did you do that?
2nd Woman:	I have suffered from bleeding for many years. I have spent all my money on doctors, none of whom could heal me. I heard of you and how you healed the sick and I believed that if only I could touch the edge of your garment I would be healed.
Jesus:	And?
2nd Woman:	As soon as I touched you I was made well instantly!
Jesus:	Daughter, your faith, your trust in me, has made you well; go in peace, and be completely healed from your sickness.

Jesus and the two disciples move on and exit from the stage

1st Woman:	Didn't I always say that if you could just touch Jesus you would be made well!
2nd Woman:	No you didn't! You didn't believe Jesus could help me.
1st Woman:	Well, I wouldn't put it exactly like that.
2nd Woman:	How would you put it then?
1st Woman:	Perhaps you happened to get well just as you touched him!
2nd Woman:	If you want to believe that you can but you'd be a fool if you did!
1st Woman:	Why?
2nd Woman:	It says in the Psalms that it is the fool who says that there is no God. I felt the power of God come from Jesus and enter my sick body. As soon as I felt the power my sickness was gone. I will never deny what God has done for me through Jesus.

The Widow's Mite

(Based upon Matthew 6:2-4, Mark 12:41-44, Luke 21:1-4)

Characters: **Peter, Matthew and Jesus**

Stage: **Single level**

Scene: **Near the Temple offering chest**

Peter: Matthew, where's Jesus?

Matthew: He's around somewhere by the money chest, Peter.

Peter: What's he doing there?

Matthew: He's watching people put money in the chest, what else would he be doing?

Peter: Why?

Matthew: How do I know? You'll have to ask him yourself.

Peter: I don't like to it seems rude.

Matthew: How come its rude to ask Jesus but not rude to bother me with questions that I don't know the answer too?

Peter: Look I didn't mean to upset you. It's just you're always making odd notes about what Jesus does and says, so I thought you would know.

Matthew: Don't you keep any notes about what he says then?

Peter: No, I keep it all up here in my head. That's fisherman's training, there's no time to look up stuff when you're fishing, besides which I'm not good at reading letters and stuff like you are.

Matthew: That's my revenue training! Everything had to be noted down.

Peter: Even the stuff under the table?

Matthew: No need to bring that up. It's all finished with now. Do you still sell short weight on your fish?

Peter: Sorry, Matthew, point taken.

Matthew: I tell you something I've noticed and that's the way people give.

Peter: How do you mean?

Matthew: Look at that fat guy at the chest now.

Peter: The one who looks like a merchant.

Matthew: That's the one, you tell me what you see.

Peter: He's taken the purse from his waist and he's holding it up. He seems to be having difficulty untying the leather ties. Ah, he's got it open now and he's holding it out and letting the coins pour out into the chest. That makes a racket, I can hear it from here! Now he's shaking the empty purse over the chest as if to shake out every last bit of gold dust. At long last he's fixing the empty purse back onto his waist and is walking away.

Matthew: Quite a performance isn't it?

Peter: Are the all like that?

Matthew: Most of them. I don't think that God is much in their thoughts when they give. They look far more interested in impressing one another!

Peter: Look there's somebody totally different going to the chest now.

Jesus enters behind Matthew and Peter so quietly they don't notice him

Matthew: She looks like a widow from her clothes.

Peter: She's not holding her purse out.

Matthew: I don't think she has one. Whatever she is giving is in her hand.

Peter: That can't be much then can it.

Matthew: Probably a lepton. That's as small as you can get!

Jesus: Actually it's two lepta Matthew!

Matthew: Oh Jesus! You made me jump!

Jesus: I'm sorry, I didn't realise you were so engrossed!

Peter: Matthew was pointing out to me the grand show most of those giving make.

Jesus: Yes, sad isn't it because they're not giving that much.

Matthew: A lot of gold has been poured into that box today, Jesus.

Jesus: Matthew if you looked at them with the eyes of your heavenly Father, rather than those of a former tax collector, you would understand.

Matthew: Understand what Jesus?

Jesus: That widow put far more money into the chest than any of the rich people who poured in gold.

Peter: How do you make that out Jesus?

Jesus: Because whilst they gave a little out of their great fortunes, she, out of her poverty, gave everything she had. In God's sight her gift was by far the greater!

Mary of Magdala

(Based upon Luke 8:2; 23-24, John 20:11-18)

Characters: Luke and Mary of Magdala

Stage: Single level

Scene: Mary's home

Luke: Mary thank you for seeing me.

Mary: James said that you are writing a history of Jesus.

Luke: Well, not really, that sounds very grand. I have undertaken to write an account of Jesus' ministry in Galilee, Jerusalem and so on. I was told that you were there from the beginning.

Mary: Not quite at the very beginning. I was not the type of person people invited to wedding feasts, even country ones like the one at Cana!

Luke: Why what were you like?

Mary: I must have given the impression of being completely mad. I didn't know what I was doing most of the time. I was driven all the time by some force outside of myself and yet inside too.

Luke: Was this how you came to meet Jesus?

Mary: In a way yes. I remember nothing about it except there was the rage inside of me then suddenly, in an instant, peace. It was the most incredible feeling. All the inner torment was gone. No outside power was driving me anymore, except…

Luke: Except what?

Mary: Well, where there had been anguish and fear, now there was love. But when I looked at Jesus it wasn't like the love a woman has for a man it was complete devotion, as if he were God.

Luke: Did that disturb you?

Mary: Not at all because he made no demands upon me. I was told afterwards that he cast 7 evil spirits out of me. I didn't know, I was in no state to count but I did know that I was free. Free to follow Jesus and serve him the best way I could, or free not to.

Luke: So what did you do, stay or go?

Mary: There were a number of women who were following Jesus. Like me they had been healed and delivered from evil spirits by Jesus. I can't remember them all but I recall Joanna.

Luke: Why do you remember her in particular?

Mary: She was from a palace family. Her husband, Chusa, was Herod's chief steward. Another I liked very much was Susanna.

Luke: What did these women do?

Mary: Susanna and Joanna, together with me and other women, contributed money to help pay for Jesus' travels with the twelve men who were closest to him.

Luke: Are you saying that women funded Jesus' ministry?

Mary; Yes, I am, does that shock you?

Luke: The more I learn about Jesus, the more shocked I become! He seems so unconventional, so forthright, so honest and so loving.

Mary: He was all of those things. But then I am biased because he set me free. I just thank God for the day he found me.

Luke: I wanted to ask about the crucifixion. May I?

Mary: Of course, I was there, I saw everything.

Luke: What were the most memorable moments for you?

Mary: That's an impossible question to answer! You must remember that even though Jesus had told us none of us understood that he would be raised from the dead. Certainly I didn't know it was a day of victory!

Luke: I don't mean to awaken unhappy memories but is there anything that you recall that might help me?

Mary: Women wept uncontrollably in the street as he was being taken to be crucified. Jesus told them not to weep for him but for themselves and their children for what was to come it seemed as if his death would unleash things over which men would have no control.

Luke: Anything else?

Mary: The way people mocked him in his suffering. The look of pain on his face. The way he spoke to one of the criminals hanging beside him "Today you will be with me in paradise."

Luke: What for you was the pivotal moment, when you knew he had risen?

Mary: When the angels at his tomb said "He is not here he is risen!" And then, later, when I was alone, he called my name and I saw him alive!

The Loneliest Man

(Based upon Luke 19:1-10)

Characters: **Zaccheus and a "business associate", Nathan**

Stage: **Single level**

Scene: **Inside the home of Zaccheus**

Nathan: Doesn't it bother you that nobody likes you?

Zaccheus: What do you mean nobody?

Nathan: Go on then name me one person, just one who likes you!

Zaccheus: Easy! Samuel's always liked me.

Nathan: But Samuel is dead! He died six years ago!

Zaccheus: Ok! But he liked me.

Nathan: He also liked that guy who was executed for mass murder and that nasty bit of work who was caught stealing money set aside for orphans!

Zaccheus: You said nothing about character references. Besides, am I to be criticised because someone who likes me likes others of whom you don't approve?

Nathan: This has nothing to do with who I like or not. All I'm asking you is to name one person, still alive, who likes you.

Zaccheus: Ah! There's Severus, he likes me.

Nathan: Of course he does! How foolish of me to overlook the chief bloodsucker of the Romans! Dear old Severus, the tax collector of tax collectors. As you always give him twice what he expects to get, you must be top of his list. The fact that he likes you has nothing to do with the bribes you give him? Presumably he loves your witty conversation and the beauty of your singing!

Zaccheus: I can't sing. Who told you I could sing?

Nathan: Nobody, I was being funny.

Zaccheus: Well don't, I don't like jokes.

Nathan: Let's face it, apart from dead men and foreign oppressors, nobody likes you.

Zaccheus: How can you be so cruel?

Nathan: You pay me to be cruel, remember?

Zaccheus:	Oh! Yes, well, did Dimitri pay you what he owed me?
Nathan:	Yes, but lay off him for a bit; his arm will take several weeks to mend.
Zaccheus:	Did you break his arm?
Nathan:	No, he broke it himself when I pushed him down the stairs!
Zaccheus:	And you say I don't have any friends.
Nathan:	I do all right down at the tavern. I've got lots of mates there.
Zaccheus:	Hmm! Nothing but a bunch of low lifes.
Nathan:	They may be low lifes but at least they can see over the counter, which is more than you can do!
Zaccheus:	Here, take your money and get out of here. I shall be going out tomorrow.
Nathan:	I wouldn't do that, if I were you. There'll be lots of crowds out tomorrow and you might get trampled on.
Zaccheus:	Why's that?
Nathan:	Because you're so short!
Zaccheus:	I meant, why would there be crowds?
Nathan:	One of the girls at the tavern told me that this new holy man is coming to town. Some of my mates told me that he'd healed people who were deaf, blind and crippled.
Zaccheus:	That must be the wine talking!
Nathan:	No straight up, I'm on the level. Everybody will turn out to see him, mark my words!
Zaccheus:	So you think that this holy man really is a healer?
Nathan:	He's not just a healer, he's a teacher too. There's more to it than that as well. He's forgiven people their sins too.
Zaccheus:	The rabbis say that only God can do that.
Nathan:	That's as may be but this man forgives people no argument. I've seen people who say he has forgiven them. You wouldn't recognise them!
Zaccheus:	What do you mean?
Nathan:	People who were burdened with worry. Bad people, some very bad, they've dropped the sin. They're smiling; they seem free!
Zaccheus:	Free! It must be nice to be free. Smiling! It must be nice to smile.
Nathan:	Perhaps you should go out tomorrow and see this man. You never know what could happen!

The Meefirst! Man

(Based upon Luke 19:1-10)

Characters: 2 men and 1 Woman "crowd"; Jesus and Zaccheus

Stage: 2 levels, upper tier used when Zaccheus is up the tree

Scene: A crowd is waiting (stage right) in a street for Jesus, above them on the upper tier is the branch of a tree

1st Man: Watch out! Old Meefirst is coming over.

Zaccheus enters stage left, but He ignores the crowd looking around and then up, he exits left and reappears on the upper tier in the tree , where Zaccheus can be seen in the tree, while the conversation below continues.

Woman: Horrible toad! How can he work for the Romans?

2nd Man: Because he only thinks of himself, that's how!

1st Man: That's right! All he's interested in is making money.

Woman: And he's not fussy how he does it. It's disgusting how much he adds on the taxes. I wonder what's brought him crawling out of his hole today?

2nd Man: Same reason as us I suppose.

1st Man: You must be joking! There's no way he'd dare show his face to the teacher.

Woman: That's right, Zaccheus thinks he's the most important person around here.

2nd Man: Well, don't you think he'd want to suss out the opposition?

1st Man: Opposition! Opposition! Are you barmy or something? Wherever Jesus goes he brings smiles and happiness. Since when has Zaccheus ever done that?

2nd Man: But he's only human…

Woman: Are you sure of that?

2nd Man: Come on, he may be hated, self-centred, greedy and horrible but he must be as curious as we are to see Jesus.

1st Man: If he does see Jesus I bet he'll be sorry.

Woman: Why?

1st Man: I reckon that Jesus would give him a piece of his mind for ripping off his fellow countrymen.

2nd Man: Hmm! Then I don't think you know much about Jesus. From what I've heard he forgives sinners rather than giving them a good kicking!

Woman: It won't happen either way because Zaccheus has disappeared but here comes Jesus.

The three start waving as Jesus enters stage left, but He ignores them and looks up, where Zaccheus can be seen in the tree.

1st Man: Do you see who's up that tree?

Woman: Why it's Zaccheus!

1st Man: Now you'll hear something! I tell you that Jesus is going to sort him out good and proper!

Jesus: Zaccheus! Zaccheus! Come down from your tree! Hurry up! I must come and stay with you today!

Zaccheus: Me Lord! Yes Lord! Right away Lord!

Zaccheus climbs down from his tree and reappears by Jesus, entering stage left

1st Man: Well, would you credit it! Jesus is going to be the guest of that rotten old sinner!

Woman: I can't believe it what could Jesus have to do with such a wicked man?

Zaccheus: Lord Jesus, I give half of all I own to the poor. And if I've taken anything from anyone by false accusation, I will restore it fourfold!

JESUS: *Taking hold of Zaccheus's arms or shoulders.* Zaccheus, today salvation has come to your household, for I, the Son of Man, have come to seek and save that which was lost.

Jesus and Zaccheus exit stage left

1st Man: I just don't understand!

2nd Man: What did I tell you? Jesus hasn't come to condemn people but to give them an opportunity to get right with God. Even people like wicked Zaccheus can be forgiven, if they are really sorry.

What a Fuss!

(Based upon John 2:15,16)

Characters: **A cow and 2 sheep**

Stage: **Single level**

Scene: **A street outside Jerusalem**

A cow and 2 sheep are pausing to take a breath after escaping from the Temple in Jerusalem.

Cow: Phew! What a commotion!

1st Sheep: Yes, I've never seen anything like it!

2nd Sheep: It's amazing to think that if all had gone according to plan I'd have been toast 5 minutes ago!

Cow: Life is wonderful!

2nd Sheep: Especially when it doesn't go according to plan!

1st Sheep: Who was that man?

Cow: I don't know but he came just in time to save my neck.

2nd Sheep: We mustn't stay here too long. They're bound to search outside the city walls soon.

1st Sheep: What could have made that man start turning all the tables over?

Cow: He was shouting something but I didn't catch what it was.

1st Sheep: It was something like "My Father's house is a house of prayer but you have made it into a den of thieves."

Cow: Did you see the faces of the dove sellers when all the birds flew off!

2nd Sheep: And all the moneychangers, when the coins went spinning over the pavement!

1st Sheep: You wouldn't think that one man could cause such a fuss would you?

Cow: And we owe him our lives!

1st Sheep: Do you think he will make a lasting difference?

2nd Sheep: What do you mean?

1st Sheep: Wouldn't it be really cool if none of us sheep or oxen would ever have to be killed in sacrifice again!

Cow: Yes but I can't see that time ever coming.

1st Sheep: Why not?

Cow: Work it out for yourself. To do away with sacrifices you'd need a fantastic, all embracing, forever, for all-time, perfect sacrifice to take the place of all the sacrifices that otherwise would have to be made.

2nd Sheep: I don't think I understood any of that!

Cow: Let me put it another way. Where are you going to find an ox or sheep better than all the millions that have already been sacrificed over thousands of years?

1st Sheep: You mean you'd need to have a different order of animal to make the one perfect sacrifice that could do away with all the other animal sacrifices?

Cow: That's right. In fact an animal probably wouldn't do.

2nd Sheep: You're not suggesting a man are you?

Cow: Difficult I know. From what we've seen of men you'd never find a perfect one anyway. Most camels have got more integrity and are certainly a lot more useful!

1st Sheep: What about the man we saw today?

Cow: The one who cleared out the Temple?

2nd Sheep: I don't want to disturb you two but we ought to start making tracks if we are to make good our escape. Whoever that man was he gave me a chance of a new life and I for one don't intend to waste it!

Who Will Be First?

(Based John 8:1-11)

Characters: Jesus and 3 men; 1 woman

Stage: Single level

Scene: Outdoors in the temple courtyard

Three men come in and stand before Jesus pushing a woman in front of them. The woman stands with her head hanging down in shame.

1st Man: Jesus! Jesus! Take a look at this wretched woman!

2nd Man: Yes, she has done a very bad thing that deserves the death penalty!

3rd man: What we want to know is what do you say about?

Jesus turns away from the men and moves away from where they are.

1st Man: I think that's got him really stumped!

2nd Man: Yes! If Jesus says she should die that'll screw him up with the Romans because only they can sentence people to death!

3rd man: On the other hand if he says she shouldn't die then everybody will see that he doesn't support his own people's customs and…

1st Man: They'll turn against him! Ha! Ha! He's not going to slip out of this one lads!

2nd Man: Jesus! Don't want to rush you or anything but can we have an answer?

3rd man: Yes, we've not had a chance to look for the rocks yet for the stoning, so hurry up!

1st Man: If you don't know what to say that's all right just tell us!

2nd Man: But don't hang around any longer we've got a lot to do today apart from dealing with this woman.

3rd man: Yeah! Life goes on for some of us, if not for her!

1st/2nd men: Ha, ha, ha! Nice one!

Jesus turns around to face the woman and the men

Jesus: Go ahead and kill her…

1st Man: Righty ho! Come on lads…

Jesus: BUT!

1st Man: But what?

Jesus: But let those who have never sinned kill her. That's what.

The men look at each other

1st Man: Hmm! Wasn't expecting that.

2nd Man: What do you think?

3rd man: I think we're stuffed, well and truly stuffed!

Silently the men leave one after another

Jesus: *Speaking to the woman.* Where have your accusers gone? Didn't even one stay to condemn you?

The woman lifts her head and looks around

Woman: No one has stayed to condemn me, Lord.

Jesus: I don't condemn you either.

Woman: Thank you, Lord.

Jesus: Go away free but don't sin again.

The Fish's Mouth

(Based on Matthew 17:24-27)

Characters: Peter and Matthew

Stage: Single level

Scene : The beach at Capernaum

Matthew:	Hello Peter! What are you doing here? I'd thought you be at the house with Jesus.
Peter:	I've just come from there.
Matthew:	Right! So what are you doing here?
Peter:	Just something for Jesus.
Matthew:	What's that in your hand?
Peter:	My hand?
Matthew:	Yes, that thing at the end of your arm.
Peter:	Oh this!
Matthew:	That's right, what are you hiding?
Peter:	Nothing!
Matthew:	That looks like a fishing line to me. Oh Peter you're not going back on your word about leaving fishing to follow Jesus?
Peter:	Of course not. It's like I told you, Jesus asked me to come down here.
Matthew:	Why is that? It can't be for fish because we've got plenty of food at the house.
Peter:	Well that's where you're wrong!
Matthew:	You mean there is no food at the house?
Peter:	No there's plenty of food there.
Matthew:	Then why are you here on the beach?
Peter:	Look Matthew, be a good chap and push off. There's something private I'm doing for Jesus and…
Matthew:	That doesn't sound like Jesus, having secrets. I've never met anybody more open than Jesus; what are you up to?
Peter:	Look I'm not up to anything, just leave me in peace.
Matthew:	It's just that you look so shifty. Come on, you can tell me.
Peter:	Well, to tell the truth I'm embarrassed.
Matthew:	About what?

Peter:	About what Jesus asked me to do.
Matthew:	Well I've not known Jesus to embarrass people, what's happened?
Peter:	The Temple tax collectors came asking me about whether Jesus paid the Temple tax or not.
Matthew:	What did you say?
Peter:	I said yes. Then I went and told Jesus.
Matthew:	What happened then?
Peter:	Jesus said some stuff, I don't think I understood everything he said and then he tells me to get the money to pay the Temple tax for him and me.
Matthew:	Now I understand you've come down here to catch some fish and sell them to raise the tax money!
Peter:	No Matthew, I have come to collect the tax money.
Matthew:	You mean you're going beach combing to find loose change people have dropped?
Peter:	No. This is the bit I find embarrassing.
Matthew:	Which bit?
Peter:	The bit where Jesus told me what to do!
Matthew:	And what did Jesus ask you to do?
Peter:	He said go down to the beach, throw in a line and open the mouth of the first fish you catch. The fish will have a coin in its mouth that will pay the Temple tax for both Jesus and me.
Matthew:	This I must see for myself!
Peter:	Matthew! It's bad enough having to do this without having an audience.
Matthew:	Look I'll stay here and you go over there. When you've caught the fish you can call me.
Peter:	Well all right but don't come until I call you.
Matthew:	I wouldn't dream of it. *Peter exits*
	I wonder how long it'll take him? There he goes throwing in the line. Hello! It looks as if he's caught something, perhaps it's just a Roman sandal!
Peter:	*His voice calls from off-stage.* Matthew, come quickly! You'll never guess what I've caught and it's got a coin in it's mouth!

A Super-duper Day!

(Based upon John 16:5-7, Acts 3:1-26)

Characters: Joshua, Bartimaeus, Benjamin, Peter and John

Stage: Single level

Scene 1: A street in Jerusalem   **Scene 2:** By the Beautiful Gate

Scene 1: *A street in Jerusalem*

Joshua: Hey! Hello Bartimaeus!

Bartimaeus: Why, if it isn't Joshua! How are you doing and what brings you to Jerusalem?

Joshua: I'm well thank you. Actually, very well. I've picked up a contract to supply sacrificial doves to the temple. I made my first delivery yesterday. What about you?

Bartimaeus: I'm still at work in the tannery. It's smelly work but steady.

Joshua: What about old whats 'is name. You know that cripple you used to help.

Bartimaeus: You mean Benjamin?

Joshua: That's right!

Bartimaeus: I still help him.

Joshua: I'm surprised that he didn't get healed by that teacher who visited Jerusalem.

Bartimaeus: You mean that man from Nazareth in Galilee? He was crucified.

Joshua: I didn't know that but then so many get crucified these days. What had he done wrong?

Bartimaeus: Search me. I heard him speak once and he seemed all right to me. But you know Jerusalem, get on the wrong side of the wrong people and you're history! Look Abe can't help me with Benjamin this morning, would you give me a hand to carry him to the Beautiful Gate?

Joshua: Of course I will, where is he living?

Bartimaeus: Just over there, come on!

Both exit stage left

Scene 2: *By the Beautiful Gate*

Benjamin: Joshua, thanks a lot for helping Bartimaeus, and for staying with me.

Joshua:	It's a pleasure to help an old friend but I must go now. It looks as if you've got customers on the way! Those two are making a beeline for you! Goodbye.
Benjamin:	Goodbye Joshua!

Joshua exits stage right

Peter and John enter stage left and keep back from Benjamin

Peter:	John, have you got any money?
John:	No, why?
Peter:	I wanted to give some to that beggar.
John:	Is that what Jesus would have done?
Peter:	Hmm! I suppose not.
John:	So what are you going to do?
Peter:	Do what Jesus would have done!

Peter and John move towards Benjamin

Benjamin:	Spare change! Any spare change?
Peter:	Look at us! I've got no silver or gold to give you.
Benjamin:	Well that makes two of us!
Peter:	But what I have I give you! Rise and walk in the name of Jesus!

Peter and John bend down to help Benjamin to his feet

Benjamin:	Wow! I can stand! I can jump! I can walk! Hallelujah!
John:	Walk with us into the Temple.
Benjamin:	This is wonderful! How did you do it?
Peter:	Your healing has not come from me. You have been healed by the power of the name of Jesus, God's anointed one.
Benjamin:	Was that the Jesus who was crucified not so long ago?
Peter:	Yes, but God raised Him from the dead. Jesus is alive and has healed you today.
Peter:	Let me just rest on your arms. What a super-duper day! I've never had a day like this in my life.
John:	But then you've never been prayed for in the name of Jesus before have you?
Benjamin:	No, I haven't. But praise God for you both and for new life in Jesus!

Wizard That Was

(Based upon Acts 10:38-43 and Acts 13:4-12)

Characters: Sergius Paulus the Roman Proconsul of Cyprus, Elymas a wizard,
                  Saul and Barnabas.

Stage: Single level

Scene: A room in the palace of Sergius Paulus.

Sergius: Good morning Elymas! I'm glad you could come.

Elymas: Dear Proconsul you well know that I always have time for you. I'm
                  honoured to be called into your illustrious presence. I bow and do
                  obeisance before your exulted person! *Elymas bows very low.*

Sergius: Yes, very nice but do get up! You have been kind enough to give me the
                  benefit of your wisdom in the past and I have two guests this morning
                  that I would like you to meet.

Elymas: Who are they most noble Proconsul?

Sergius: They are called Saul and Barnabas. Since arriving in Cyprus they have
                  been talking about a person who has done great and powerful things
                  past imagining.

Elymas: Another like myself! How could this be majestic one?

Sergius: That's why I thought it would be a good idea for you to meet them. If
                  these men are not being honest I'm sure that you will find them out.

Elymas: Serene Proconsul, I'm deeply moved by your trust in your poor servant!

Sergius: You have a reputation for great powers Elymas, such a one is invaluable
                  in situations like this.

Elymas: Ah beloved Proconsul you are, as ever, correct! It is true that I am
                  invaluable and have incalculable worth to your good self. I will protect
                  you from any that would dare to beguile you with lies and fanciful tales.

Sergius: Well, here's your opportunity, they're coming in now.

Enter Saul and Barnabas

Saul: Proconsul greetings! My name is Saul and this is my companion
                  Barnabas.

Sergius: Welcome, Saul, welcome Barnabas! This gentleman is Elymas an
                  adviser of mine. Now to business! I understand that you tell of a man who
                  has done great and powerful things. Tell me about him.

Saul: Sir, I will gladly tell you about this person, his name is Jesus from the town of Nazareth in Galilee. The one true and living God anointed this Jesus of Nazareth with the Holy Spirit and with power. Jesus went about doing good, and healing everybody whom the devil had made sad. God worked through Jesus in such a way that he healed the sick and the lame, gave the blind their sight, the deaf their hearing and the mute their voices. Jesus was arrested on false charges and Pontius Pilate was persuaded to permit his death. Jesus was crucified, died and was buried in a sealed tomb. However, three days later, God raised him from the dead and he spoke, walked and ate with many people. This Jesus has been appointed by God to be judge of all, the living and the dead. But everyone who believes in Jesus can have their sins forgiven, be filled with God's Holy Spirit and receive everlasting life.

Elymas: Honourable Proconsul, this is nothing but a tissue of lies. A dead man raised from the dead! Your very reason tells you such things can't be!

Saul: Elymas you are the one who lies against the truth! You are a son of the devil, an enemy of all that is good and the Lord will strike you blind for a time as a punishment!

Elymas: Aaah! Proconsul, I cannot see! Help me there is nothing but darkness before me!

Sergius: What magic is this that you have worked Saul?

Saul: No magic Sir. God loves you and wants you to hear and know the truth about his son Jesus. He will not allow this wretch to stand in the way of your salvation!

Sergius: Lead me to this Jesus, Saul, so that I may learn from him. But what of Elymas?

Saul: His sight will return to him when God wills it. And if he truly repents of his wicked ways and wizardry he will be forgiven too. For the time being don't be concerned about him. Elymas has no powers that can hurt you; he is the wizard that was!

Whoops!

(Based on Acts 17:24-27)

Characters: Paul, Luke, Eutychus and a man and a woman

Stage: Lower Level: A street   Upper Level: A house

Scene: A body lies in the street, people are upstairs in the house.

Paul and Luke are upstairs in the house and a man and woman are looking at the body in the street

Woman: Eutychus! Eutychus! Can you hear us?

Man: Look at the angle of his head, I don't like it!

Woman: Well I don't suppose you'd look so smart if you'd just fallen three floors!

Man: I mean, I think he's dead!

Woman: Not Eutychus! Oh Eutychus! Wake up!

Man: I'm going to get Paul.

Woman: You can't disturb Paul. He's in the middle of teaching!

Man: If Paul hadn't gone on so long in that stuffy room Eutychus wouldn't have got drowsy and fallen out of the window!

Woman: How can you say that?

Man: Easily, watch my lips. If Paul hadn't…

Woman: All right go and get Paul if you must.

Man: Dr. Luke is with him, may be he'll be able to help but I fear Eutychus is dead.

Woman: Oh Eutychus please don't die! Please hurry and get the Doctor.

The man exits and reappears on the upper level of the stage. Below the woman prays silently by the body

Man: Paul, Paul, please come quickly. Eutychus has fallen from the window and is dead!

Paul: How on earth did that happen?

Man: He was listening to you talking and fell asleep.

Paul: How flattering! Luke does it not say somewhere in the scriptures "be sure your sins will find you out!"

Luke: Absolutely, Moses wrote it in the Book of Numbers. However, I think you will find that the context refers to people who promise to do something then break their word, rather than applying to those who fall asleep during preaching.

Paul:	Interesting Doctor, interesting. So then if this Eutychus has not fallen from sin there is hope!
Luke:	We have seen the Lord work miracles before.
Paul:	We have indeed.
Man:	Gentlemen he lies down stairs in a bad way, could we hurry please?
Paul:	But you say he's dead. Luke as a physician I would welcome your opinion in this matter. If a person is dead is it necessary to rush to the body?
Luke:	I can't think of any particular reason why, it is midnight after all so we are not troubled by the sun's rays hastening decomposition and the release of unpleasant odours.
Paul:	I thought that would be so.
Luke:	However, for the well being of this kind gentleman who has brought this tragedy to our attention it would be best to go down now.
Man:	Thank you Doctor let me lead the way.

The man, Paul and Luke exit the upper level and enter the lower level moving towards the body

Luke:	*Speaking to the praying woman.* Please allow us to see the young man my dear.
Woman:	He's not dead is he sir?
Paul:	*Bending over the body.* Don't worry, the breath of life is in him. Luke give me a hand to lift him up.
Luke:	Eutychus can you hear me?
Eutychus:	Where am I? What happened?
Paul:	You fell asleep while I was preaching and fell out of the window!
Eutychus:	Really?
Paul:	Really!
Eutychus:	But you're so interesting, how could I have done that?
Paul:	That is a total mystery to me too! But I'll tell you one thing everybody in the whole world will know about it soon.
Eutychus:	How so?
Paul:	Because if I know my good friend Dr. Luke here, he will find it an irresistible story to add to the diary that he hopes to publish! I can see the heading now, "Apostle bores person to death!"

I Told You So!

(Based on Acts 27)

Characters: Paul, Luke and Julius (Captain of the Imperial Regiment of Rome)

Stage: 1/2 levels (2nd level can be used for effects such as sail etc.)

Scene 1: On board ship in a gale   **Scene 2:** A beach on Malta

Scene 1:   *On board ship in a gale*

Luke appears on stage first he turns and greets Paul as he enters

Luke:	Good morning Paul!
Paul:	Is it?
Luke:	Oh dear! Didn't we sleep well?
Paul:	Well enough but it was interrupted by a dream.
Luke:	What was it about?
Paul:	This voyage.
Luke:	Oh!
Paul:	Sometimes I wonder about you! Here we are, miles from land in the middle of a storm and you're super calm!
Luke:	Remember all the time I spent interviewing eyewitnesses of Jesus? If I learnt one thing it's don't panic!
Paul:	You know me, Luke, you know I don't panic.
Luke:	That's true Paul, but you do get excited!

Captain Julius enters

Julius:	Ave Paul! Salve Doctor! Both well I trust.
Paul:	As well as one can be in the middle of a storm.
Julius:	There's no need to be concerned, the sailors have assured me that it will blow itself out before long. They have been travelling these waters for years and…
Paul:	They don't know what they are doing! I warned you at Fair Havens but you didn't listen to me. Listen now, last night I had a dream…
Julius:	So what? I didn't sleep that well myself!
Luke:	Captain, I think you'd better listen to Paul, this storm is getting worse.
Paul:	My dream was from God and He warned me that the ship will be lost and its cargo but that all 276 on board will be saved.
Julius:	Anything else?

Paul:	Just keep an eye on the sailors. I promise you at the first opportunity they'll try and make off in the lifeboat.
Julius:	Thank you Paul, I'll remember what you've said.
Scene 2:	*A beach on Malta*

Luke enters the stage apparently looking for someone. Paul is slumped over

Luke:	Paul! Paul! Is that you?
Paul:	Yes, Luke it's me. Do you know this is my third shipwreck.
Luke:	Really? Well, I don't suppose you ever get used to them.
Paul:	No, each one has a unique feature. Right now I'm frozen!
Luke:	Come along, the locals have lit a fire to warm us all up.
Paul:	All?
Luke:	It's just as your dream foretold. The ship and cargo is a total loss but not one of the passengers or crew have been lost. Look here comes Captain Julius. *Julius enters.*
Julius:	Ave Doctor! So you've found the hero of the hour have you?
Luke:	Yes, but I want to get him warmed up by the fire as quickly as possible.
Julius:	Of course, let me give you some help. Ave Paul! Thanks to your warning not a single person was lost!
Paul:	You flatter me Captain. It was the Lord who warned me and all the credit must go to him.
Julius:	About your Lord, there are men who say that he is dead.
Paul:	He was crucified some time ago in Jerusalem under Pontius Pilate. Your soldiers made no mistakes, he died and was buried.
Julius:	But you say your Lord talks to you, he can't be dead!
Paul:	No, Captain Julius, he can't be dead and he isn't. Father God raised him from the dead on the third day. Many, many people saw him, spoke with him and ate with him before he returned to heaven. You talk to the good Doctor here, he interviewed people who knew Jesus.
Julius:	Doctor, you must tell me more about this Jesus. By the way I have your writing case here, it was saved by one of my men.
Luke:	Praise God! I was making notes of Paul's journeys but I thought I'd lost them. Now I can finish the record of our adventures!

Take This Down!

(Based on 2 Corinthians 1:1 & 11:16-12:16)

Characters: Paul and Timothy

Stage: Single level

Scene: A room

Timothy is at a writing desk with reed pen and roll of papyrus, Paul is standing by him

Timothy: So what are you going to say to them?

Paul: Our Corinthian friends you mean?

Timothy: Yes. We know that they've been listening to men who are fooling them with their boasting by saying how good they are.

Paul: I'm going to have to expose them for what they are. I don't want to do it but I see no other way. They need to understand what it really means to be a true follower of Jesus.

Timothy: So you'll tell them?

Paul: Yes, so I'll tell them.

Timothy: How shall I begin?

Paul: Oh the usual way. You know, "This letter is from Paul, appointed by God to be an apostle of Christ Jesus." Wait a minute; make sure you put in your name too. Sosthenes wrote the last letter I sent to them and if you don't put your name in someone could well claim it's a forgery, especially if they don't like what's in it!

Timothy: So what shall I write?

Paul: Do you remember what I said to you this morning about the comfort God gives?

Timothy: Yes, I think so.

Paul: Well it would be a good way to start the letter…

Timothy: …To break them in gently you mean?

Paul: Exactly! I think you'd better follow that up by telling them why I changed my plans to visit them.

Timothy: Right, I'll check those sections with you when I've written them. Now what do you want to say about those deceivers?

Paul: Tell them I'm a fool but that I shall boast too!

Timothy: OK, what are you going to boast about?

Paul:	Well, those deceivers in Corinth say that they are really of God's chosen people the Hebrews, true descendants of Abraham and that they are servants of Jesus. Well, Timothy you write that I too am all those things.
Timothy:	Paul, why are you smiling? What are you thinking, what are you up to?
Paul:	Smiling? Me? What am I up to? Really, I don't know what you mean! But let me ask you some questions Timothy. Yes and, as you answer them, write down your answers in the letter!
Timothy:	Fire away, Paul!
Paul:	Tell me Timothy, do I work hard serving Jesus and telling people about Him?
Timothy:	Why, nobody has worked harder!
Paul:	Then write that down! What about prison?
Timothy:	You should know all about that! You've been there more than any other Christian I know!
Paul:	Then write that down! What about being whipped?
Timothy:	You should know all about that! You've been given 39 lashes five times and beaten with rods three times. And you were stoned and left for dead!
Paul:	Then write that down! What about shipwrecks?
Timothy:	You should know all about that! You've been shipwrecked twice and spent a whole day and night adrift in the sea!
Paul:	Shipwrecked three times, actually, write that down! What about travels on land?
Timothy:	You should know all about that! You've trudged for mile after mile; you've run the risks of floods; robbers; Jews and others who hated you, including those who said they were Christians but were not!
Paul:	Then write that down! What about endurance?
Timothy:	You should know all about that! You've kept going when tired, weak, in pain, hungry, thirsty and cold!
Paul:	Then write that down! We need to tell Christians that they should endure suffering as a good soldier of Jesus Christ and learn that they can work through everything with his help.

The Soil

(Based upon Matthew 13:3-9 and 18-23)

Characters: An off-stage Narrator, 1 or more birds, 1 flower, 2 hands wearing green gloves and "peepers", 3 sacks, one marked with '30', another marked with '60' and the third marked with '100' (these should be cut out of strong card and mounted on wooden strips or doweling so they can be lifted up)

Stage: Single level

Scene: A plain stage or one with a backdrop of a field

Narrator: A farmer went out to sow some seed. As he scattered his seed some fell on the path by his field. But the birds came down and gobbled up the seed on the path.

Birds: *The birds enter and peck at the seed on the path field*

Narrator: That path is just like people who hear the good news about Jesus but don't understand it, so Satan comes and snatches the word of God from their hearts.

Birds: *The birds leave*

Narrator: Some of the farmer's seed fell down upon shallow soil that lay on top of rock. The seed sprouted and grew quickly!

Flowers: *The flower springs up and shouts.* Hooray! Hooray! What a sunny day!

Narrator: Unfortunately, in spite of the promising start, the plant soon wilted and died away because there was not enough food or water in the shallow soil. The shallow soil is just like those who are very excited when they first hear about Jesus but as soon as they face problems and challenges they fade away because they have not bothered to read the Bible and pray.

Flowers: *The flower wilts downward out of sight*

Narrator: But the farmer had sown more seed, although it had fallen amongst weeds.

Flowers: *The Flower springs up and looks around.* Oh! Hello who are you?

Hands: *The hands come up beside the plant.* Weed! Weed!

Narrator: Regretfully the weeds grew up and strangled the farmer's plant!

Hands: *The hands strangle the Flower, which chokes.* Hee! Hee! Weed!

Flower:	Aaah! *The flower sinks down out of the grasp of the hands, which look down waving goodbye but remain in position.*
Narrator:	The weedy soil is just like those who hear and accept the good news about Jesus but then allow the cares of life and the love of money to crowd him out of their lives.
Hands:	*The hands look at the audience then sink down waving goodbye.*
Narrator:	However, the farmer had sown more seed, this time in good soil.
Flower:	*The flower grows up slowly and stands tall and strong.*
Narrator:	The good soil is just like the hearts of all those who really receive the good news about Jesus in their heart.
Flower:	*The flower exits.*
Narrator:	You can tell by the way they live that Jesus is real to them and they are eager to do want he wants. They read the Bible, pray and are a blessing to those around them.
Sacks:	*Hold up the '30', '60' & '100' fold sacks in time to the narrator's final line.*
Narrator:	And they produce a large harvest of fruit in their lives, 30, 60 and even 100 times as much as has been planted in their lives!

The Farmer

(Based upon Matthew 13:24-30 and 36-43)

Characters: **Man and girl; a Farmer, his servant and his enemy.**

Stage: **2 levels: Top level – father tells his daughter (Sophie) a story.**

                   Lower level – the story is played out.

Scene: **Lower level is a field.**

On the top level a father tells his daughter a story

Father: Sophie did you know that the Kingdom of Heaven is like a farmer who planted good seed?

Sophie: No, I didn't.

Father: Well it is, listen…

The farmer is speaking to his servant

Servant: Well, sir we've finished sowing all the good seed in your field.

Farmer: All of it, already?

Servant: Yes sir, every last one.

Farmer: Excellent news! Well you'd better go and tell the men to take a rest. Come to think of it you'd better have a rest as well!

Servant: Thank you sir, it's been a very long day.

Both servant and farmer exit

Sophie: Who is the farmer in the story?

Father: The farmer is Jesus and the field is the world.

Sophie: What about the good seed?

Father: The good seeds are Christians. But there is more to the story because that night an enemy of the farmer crept into the field…

The farmer's enemy sneaks into the field

Enemy: Now is my chance! All of them are sleeping like babes and no one left on guard! Let's make sure we cover the entire area with weed seeds!

Father: So, the Farmer's enemy did his dirty work sowing weed seeds all over the field!

The enemy moves slowly across the stage sowing seeds then exits

Sophie: Who is the enemy?

Father: That's the devil.

Sophie: What happens next, did the farmer find out about the weed seeds?

Father: No one found out about them until some time later…

The farmer's servant shows him the field full of weeds.

Servant: Just look at that sir?

Farmer: But that's terrible!

Servant: I know sir. None of us can work out why the field is so full of weeds!

Farmer: What about the crop?

Servant: The crop is there but the weeds have grown up amongst it.

Farmer: How strange! An enemy must have done this.

Servant: Shall I get the men to pull the weeds out, sir?

Farmer: No you mustn't do that! Let the weeds grow up with the crop. If you pull up the weeds now you will damage the wheat because there is always the possibility that you will pull both up together.

Servant: But what shall we do?

Farmer: When it comes to harvest, tell the men to sort out the weeds from the wheat. Then we'll be able to burn up the weeds and put the wheat safely into the barn.

Both servant and farmer exit.

Father: Sophie, can you guess what the harvest represents in the story?

Sophie: I'm not sure.

Father: Well, the harvest is the end of the world and the people collecting the harvest are angels.

Sophie: But what does it all mean?

Father: It's like a picture of what will happen at the end of the world. Jesus will send his angels and they will remove from the Church everything that causes sin and all those who do evil and they will throw them into the furnace and burn them.

Sophie: You mean just like the weeds are burnt up?

Father: Yes, but the godly, the ones who are like the wheat in the story, will shine like the sun in the Kingdom of God.

Sophie: Is that why sometimes bad things happen now in the Church?

Father: Yes, because the devil has sown his people in amongst those who are true believers.

Sophie: That's scary!

Father: Not really because Jesus has it all under control. As you can see from the story those who do evil will not get away with it!

The Fisherman

(Based upon Matthew 13:47-51)

Characters: **Rueben, Nathan and Zach**

Stage: **Single level**

Scene: **By the shore of Lake Galilee**

Two men are helping a fisherman sort his catch into boxes

Reuben: Nathan, Zach, thank you for helping me like this.

Nathan: I'm not sure it will be help, neither of us has ever sorted fish before.

Zach: That's true but when your Sarah told us Ben was sick we thought you might need help.

Reuben: Well I do and I'm very grateful. Before we start, pull those boxes over here and I'll show you what to do.

Nathan and Zach go to the side of the stage to "pull" some boxes back to the middle

Zach: Hey, Nathan, do you know what one fish said to the other fish on the fishmongers slab?

Nathan: No, what did one fish say to another fish on the fishmonger's slab?

Zach: You must be gutted!

Nathan: Have you got any more?

Zach: Yes!

Nathan: Well keep them to yourself.

Reuben: OK! This is what to do. Any fish that look like this are good so put them in this box. But any that look like that, put in that box. Now ones that look like this we'll put in this box here. Anything else throw over there and we'll get rid of them later.

Nathan: So the boxes are used for the good fish?

Reuben: That's right.

Zach: Nathan, if you hear a round of applause do you not what you'll have found?

Nathan: No.

Zach: A starfish!

Reuben: Is he always like this, Nathan?

Nathan: More often than not. He always makes a joke of everything, don't you Zach.

Zach:	Well my old mum always said that if you didn't laugh you'd cry!
Reuben:	That's OK Zach but there are some things that are not so funny.
Zach:	Like what?
Reuben:	Like stuff I heard that preacher talking about.
Nathan:	You mean the one who has healed people?
Reuben:	That's the one.
Zach:	What was he talking about, Reuben?
Reuben:	In a funny sort of a way he was talking about us!
Nathan:	What do you mean? I've not met him!
Reuben:	He was talking about the end of the world.
Zach:	That's not very cheerful!
Nathan:	Shut-up Zach! What did he say?
Reuben:	He said that the Kingdom of Heaven was like a net thrown into the sea and catches fish of every kind. Then when the net is full the fishermen drag it up onto the shore.
Zach:	Then what?
Reuben:	The men then sort the good fishes into boxes and throw away the bad ones.
Nathan:	Just like we're doing, you mean?
Reuben:	Yes, just like we're doing!
Zach:	But what was the point of what he said?
Reuben:	He said that in the same way at the end of the world the angels would come and separate the wicked people from the godly people.
Zach:	And what happens to the wicked people?
Reuben:	Oh, they'll be thrown into the fire.
Nathan:	Did he say what made a person godly?
Reuben:	A godly person is one who is truly sorry for all the bad things that they've done and asks God's forgiveness and obeys the teachings of this preacher.
Zach:	You mean what's 'is name?
Reuben:	That's right, Jesus of Nazareth.
Nathan:	What do you want us to do with all the bad fish, Reuben?
Reuben:	Throw them on a fire and burn them up, otherwise they'll stink!
Zach:	Ouch!

The Mustard Seed

(Based upon Matthew 31:31-32)

Characters: A giant runner bean seed, a small round mustard seed, Cut -out flowerpots of different sizes. *(These can be cutout prop figures, the commentary is given by a single narrator who can either be off-stage or an on-stage "human" puppet).*

Stage: **Single level** *(If using a puppet as the narrator it can be used on a second upper level.)*

Scene: **A potting shed bench.**

Narrator: Once upon a time there was a runner bean seed.

Runner bean seed comes on stage.

Narrator: The runner bean was a large handsome seed and he knew it! He would often tell other seeds, "When you are a runner bean seed it gives one a certain presence in the potting shed. You are, how can I put it, noticeable and noticed."

He would also say that, "He who has been created a runner bean seed has won first prize in the seed packet of life!"

Of course, like all the other seeds he was waiting for the day when he would be planted and fulfil the destiny to which all seeds are called, to produce a plant and many more seeds like himself.

Amongst the other seeds in the potting shed was a mustard seed.

Mustard seed comes on stage

Narrator: The mustard seed was a humble little seed. The runner bean seed said that this was because, "He had much to be humble about!"

The only thing that puzzled the runner bean was why the little mustard seed was kept in a container all by himself. The reason was that the gardener to whom the potting shed belonged treasured that little seed and didn't want to lose him. One day there was a commotion in the potting shed and flowerpots of different sizes began to appear.

Different sized flowerpots come on stage

Narrator: The runner bean looked at the pots with interest. "I wonder which will be my new home?" He thought. Poor bean! Like anybody with a high opinion of himself he was very self-centred and always thought everything was organised for his benefit! On the other hand the humble mustard seed saw the flowerpots but never dreamt any would be for him. The gardener chose one special flowerpot and put the others away.

All flowerpots except one leave the stage

"Now where's that seed?" Said the gardener.

"I'm over here!" the runner bean called out. But the gardener didn't hear because just at that moment his wife came in.

"Where's this seed you wanted me to see?" She asked.

The gardener picked up the special container holding the mustard seed.

"Look at that, it's a mustard seed! Isn't it tiny, especially when you compare it to something like this runner bean seed."

The runner bean seed exits

Before he could get over the shock of being called a "something" the runner bean seed was picked up by a grubby finger and thumb and thrust towards the gardener's wife. "What are you going to do with it?" She said.

The gardener dropped the runner bean seed back onto the bench.

The runner bean comes back on stage

Narrator: "I shall plant the mustard seed in this flowerpot." The gardener replied.

The mustard seed appears by the flowerpot

"Jack told me that as far as he can tell this is the type of seed Jesus talked about in his parable."

His wife nodded. "You mean the parable of the mustard seed? The smallest of all seeds which becomes the largest of garden plants where birds can come and rest in its branches. The one Jesus said was like the Kingdom of Heaven?"

"Yes!" Said the gardener. "So I want to give it the best possible start."

So saying the gardener planted the mustard seed in the flowerpot.

The mustard seed moves behind the flowerpot as if planted into it

The gardener's wife asked what he wanted to do with the runner bean seed. "Throw it away I've got more than I need!"

The runner bean seed exits

Now if it had been another mustard seed that would be a different story! Let's take this pot indoors."

The flowerpot with the mustard seed exits

Loading the Dough with Life

(Based upon Matthew 13:33)

Characters: **A mother and daughter (contemporary dress)**

Stage: **Single level**

Scene: **A kitchen**

Mother and daughter are in the kitchen about to make some bread

Mother:	Do you remember what I told you?
Daughter:	I think so.
Mother:	Well do you remember what I said about the yeast?
Daughter:	Yes. You said it wasn't necessary to use a lot of it in bread making.
Mother:	Do you remember why?
Daughter:	No, I can't.
Mother:	You know that bread dough on the table looks like a lump of solid stuff. But when the bread comes out of the oven it has a light texture.
Daughter:	When you slice up a loaf it looks as if it has air holes in it!
Mother:	That's it exactly, it does have air holes in it. I use yeast to put them there!
Daughter:	How does that work?
Mother:	The yeast is a type of fungus, it's actually living, not like flour. When I add yeast to my bread dough the yeast ferments by making tiny bubbles of carbon dioxide gas. The gas causes the dough to rise and make it light.
Daughter:	So that's why bread has holes in it?
Mother:	Yes! It's also why Jesus said that the Kingdom of Heaven was like yeast.
Daughter:	Is the Kingdom of Heaven full of holes then?
Mother:	No! But just like a small amount of yeast will work its way through a large amount of dough, so people who follow Jesus have affected every area of our lives. That's why Jesus told his parable.
Daughter:	How do you mean?
Mother:	In our country, schools, hospitals, caring for the poor and sick, the fight for better working conditions, the right to a fair trial, banning slavery, aid for people overseas and giving safe homes for people escaping from persecution were all started by Christians.
Daughter:	But wasn't that because there were always lots and lots of Christians in this country?
Mother:	Not really. Remember the parable of the yeast.

Daughter: You mean just as only a little yeast is needed to make the dough rise so only a few Christians are needed to make a difference to where they live.

Mother: That's right, provided the Christians are alive!

Daughter: You mean like the yeast?

Mother: Yes!

Daughter: But how do Christians stay "alive"?

Mother: By believing what God says to them through the Bible and His Holy Spirit and not just hearing what God says but actually doing it as well.

Daughter: You mean by living like Jesus?

Mother: Yes, Christians do great things not because they are in great numbers but because they serve a great God!

Treasure Hunter

(Based upon Matthew 13:44)

Characters: **A treasure hunter, farmer, friend and a wife**

Stage: **Single level**

Scene 1: **A field** **Scene 2:** **A farmhouse**

Scene 3: **A bar** **Scene 4:** **A farmhouse**

Scene 1: *A treasure hunter is sweeping a field with a metal detector.*

Man: Decent of the farmer to let me survey his fields. This doesn't look very promising though.

The metal detector starts letting off a rapid bleeping

Man: Hello! What have we here? Let's switch off the detector and dig!

The man switches off the detector and starts digging around

Man: A box! I wonder if I can get it open. There! Wow! Coins and unless I'm very much mistaken I think they're gold! Hmm! Better put them back. If this field was mine then the value of this find would come to me! I think I'd better see the farmer.

Scene 2: *The treasure hunter is talking to the farmer*

Farmer: How have you got on?

Man: Not bad, it's a bit windy out there today!

Farmer: It often is. How can I help?

Man: It's that bottom field of yours the one with the old machinery in it. Would you be willing to sell it?

Farmer: What on earth do you want it for? It's agricultural land you know, you couldn't build on it.

Man: I know but with its access from the lane I could use it to train people in the use of metal detectors.

Farmer: Well, would you want me to move the old equipment?

Man: No, it wouldn't cause me any problems.

Farmer: I don't need the field but agricultural land costs a fair bit you know. Let me think about it, discuss it with my wife and I'll get in touch.

Scene 3: *The man is sitting with a friend in a bar*

Man: So he's willing to sell if I can raise the cash.

Friend: It strikes me as being expensive for a bit of rough farmland you can't

	build on.
Man:	Well, I'm happy with the price, the only problem is raising the money.
Friend:	And you want my help? I've got no money to lend you!
Man:	I don't want your money but you could help me sell my car.
Friend:	Sell your car? You're mental; E Type Jaguars like yours are hard to come by.
Man:	Exactly and with your contacts you should be able to get a very good price for it.
Friend:	I don't understand. Does the field mean that much to you?
Man:	Yes, it does.
Friend:	OK, but I think you're balmy! I wish I could afford your E Type!
Scene 4	*The farmer is talking to his wife.*
Wife:	So he's actually bought the field then.
Farmer:	Yes, how else do you think I could afford that lovely old E Type!
Wife:	You spent all that money on a second-hand car?
Farmer:	It's an investment my dear. It's like the man in the parable who sold everything he had to by a field with a treasure hidden in it.
Wife:	Do you reckon he did sell everything?
Farmer:	In Jesus' parable, yes, the man would have done but our bloke only had to sell his E Type.
Wife:	But what about the treasure?
Farmer:	Oh, the treasure. Yes, well I only stuck it in that field as a joke. I thought it would make it more interesting for him!
Wife:	But won't he say something when he discovers it's worthless?
Farmer:	He won't say anything because when he found the box he should have told me about it.
Wife:	But have you been honest?
Farmer:	Look, I never asked him to buy the field and I certainly didn't say anything to him about buried treasure! He told me he wanted it simply to use as a training ground for treasure hunters.
Wife:	Strikes me he'd have been better off seeking the Kingdom of Heaven!
Farmer:	He's typical of so many! Always looking for a short cut to happiness when the true treasure lies above, not beneath the earth! Like a spin in the E type?

Pearl Merchant

(Based upon Matthew 13:45-46)

Characters: **Isaac and Solly and off-stage Narrator**

Stage: **Single level**

Scene: **A café**

Two men are talking together

Isaac: So why did you want to meet me Solly?

Solly: I know you like a good deal.

Isaac: A good deal? You are offering me a good deal? Since when have you ever offered anybody a good deal?

Solly: Isaac that's not kind.

Isaac: Kind it may not be but true it is!

Solly: Name just one time when I've let you down.

Isaac: Let me get my diary!

Solly: Isaac!

Isaac: Just kidding, Solly. How can I help?

Solly: I am looking to raise some cash.

Isaac: Out of necessity or for speculation?

Solly: This is not something I have to do, it's something I want to do.

Isaac: Now that's a pity.

Solly: Why?

Isaac: Well if you were desperate I know I would get a better deal!

Solly: Listen, you've always liked my rubies…

Isaac: Are you offering me your rubies?

Solly: Yes. Rubies have always been special to you and you know a lot about them, so I've come to you.

Isaac: Well, remind me of what you've got.

Solly: I have 24 star rubies between 80 and 130 carats.

Isaac: How long did it take you to collect them?

Solly: Ever since I started. As time went by I replaced inferior stones.

Isaac: What colour are they?

Solly: Pigeon's blood.

Isaac: The very best!

Solly:	Yes, but I also have a good collection of red spinels, none of which is less than 200 carats.
Isaac:	I must see them. But why do you want to get rid of them?
Solly:	Like I said I want to invest in something else.
Isaac:	Come on what is it?
Solly:	You don't deal in pearls do you?
Isaac:	No, strictly gemstones.
Solly:	Recently I've switched to pearls, I've been getting to know where the best ones come from and so on. And Isaac, I have found it!
Isaac:	Found what?
Solly:	The pearl of all pearls! Its shape is perfect and its iridescent lustre beyond description! I know that I must have it!
Isaac:	But to get rid of all those rubies for one pearl!
Solly:	You've forgotten my emeralds and sapphires. Thomas has already bought my sapphires and the Greek trader, Demetrius, is preparing an offer for my emeralds.
Isaac:	I don't believe what I'm hearing! You're selling all your gemstones for one pearl!
Solly:	It's a little more than that. I've put my house on the market.
Isaac:	You've put your house on the market! What madness is this?
Solly:	It's not madness, its passion Isaac. If you saw the pearl, you'd feel the same way!
Isaac:	I doubt it! I'm ashamed to say I don't know much about them and avoid dealing in them like the plague.
Solly:	When I get this pearl, I'll show it to you and you will be hooked for life!
Isaac:	Solly, take care! Can there be anything worth giving up all your possessions to gain?

The puppets "freeze" and after the Narrator speaks they exit

Narrator:	Jesus said that the Kingdom of Heaven is like a pearl merchant looking for choice pearls. When he found a pearl of great value, he sold everything he had and bought it!

A Fair Day's Work

(Based upon Matthew 20:1-16)

Characters: **Vineyard owner and four workers**

Stage: **Single level**

Scene: **Outside**

Three men are talking together

1st Worker: Come on Guv'nor see it from our point of view, is it fair, is it just?

2nd Worker: We started out really early and we've worked from sun-up to sundown but that guy you've just paid off only started at 9 o'clock and you paid him the full rate!

Enter a third worker

1st Worker: Yeah! Hard workers like us are hard to come by!

3rd Worker: Hello boss. What's all this fuss about?

Owner: Nothing, I just appear to have upset these two gentlemen over a small matter…

1st Worker: Small matter! Now listen…

3rd Worker: Calm down, calm down! This man's a good boss there's no reason to shout like that.

2nd Worker: How do you know and what business is it of yours anyway?

3rd Worker: I work for him…

1st Worker: Since when? I've not seen you before and I've been here all day!

3rd Worker: I was working in a different area to you. I didn't clock on until noon.

2nd Worker: And how much has he agreed to pay you then?

3rd Worker: The standard daily rate, not that it's any of your business.

1st Worker: Oh yes it is! Me and my mate here have slaved all day and for what?

Owner: The standard daily rate. That's what you agreed.

Enter a fourth worker

1st Worker: Somebody hold me back before I do him an injury!

4th Worker: Hello Sir! What's all this fuss about?

Owner: I've upset our two friends here because…

1st Worker: Friends! Friends he calls us. Oh give me strength!

4th Worker: But what's the problem?

3rd Worker: The Boss is proposing to pay these blokes the standard daily rate for a day's work. That upsets them because another bloke has been paid the same rate and he worked shorter hours.

2nd Worker: And yourself, don't forget yourself! You've only worked half a day and you're still getting the full whack!

4th Worker: Why criticise a man for being generous?

3rd Worker: That's exactly what I think!

Owner: Well I'm glad you think like that because I hired this man at 5 o'clock and I'm going to pay him exactly the same as everybody else.

3rd Worker: Come again! This man has worked for just one hour in the coolest part of the day and you're going to pay him what you pay me! That doesn't make sense.

1st Worker: What's it to you? You only worked half the time my mate and me worked; you've got no complaint.

Owner: Neither have you!

1st Worker: No complaint! How can you justify paying this bloke in effect twice as much as me and this one an unbelievable 12 times! Answer me that!

Owner: All of you freely entered into your contracts knowing the pay you would receive. Not one of you complained about the rate I offered and that is the rate you've been paid.

4th Worker: Sir, you have helped me greatly. My needs for my family are just as great as these other men and I didn't know about your hiring workers until late in the day. Thank you for your kindness.

2nd Worker: You defeat me, I just don't get it. Would it be so unreasonable for you to have used an hourly rate of pay instead of a daily rate?

Owner: If you find me hard to understand, how will you ever understand God's love because he too treats people with equal kindness regardless of what they deserve!

The Three Servants

(Based upon Matthew 25:14-30)

Characters: **A master and 3 servants**

Stage: **Single level**

Scene: **The main hall of the master's house**

A servant is in the room when a second enters it, calling the first servant

Secundus: Tertius! Tertius!

Tertius: What is it Secundus?

Secundus: Crescens says the master has returned! He will be here any minute and wants to know how we got on with the gold he left us.

Tertius: Right! I better get into the garden; did you leave the trowels by the bench?

Secundus: Yes, I did but this is no time to start gardening!

Tertius: Don't worry I won't be long.

They both exit together once they are off stage the Master enters with Crescens

Crescens: Was your journey successful Master?

Master: Very, thank you Crescens but I have been looking forward to coming home. Where are Secundus and Tertius? I am eager to find out how resourceful you have been while I was away!

Crescens: I can see Secundus coming now and I'm sure that Tertius won't be far behind.

Master: Well let's hope not!

Secundus enters

Secundus: Greetings Master! I trust your journey was profitable.

Master: It was indeed but I'm interested right now to know if you, Crescens and Tertius have had a profitable time while I've been away.

Crescens: Tertius is coming now, Master.

Master: Excellent!

Tertius enters

Master: Greetings Tertius, I am pleased that your duties didn't hold you up for too long!

Tertius: Forgive me Master…

Master: Please don't apologise, I am eager to hear what all of you have to report. Crescens, how did you get on?

Crescens: Master before you left you gave me 5 bags of gold. I have invested the money and it has now doubled in value.

Master: Well, well! You make me wish that I had put more in your care! Good man because you have been faithful with this small amount I shall you increase your responsibilities. I think we must celebrate later, don't you?

Crescens: *Bowing.* Thank you Master!

Master: Secundus, your turn now. How did you get on?

Secundus: Master, you gave me 2 bags of gold and like Crescens I have now doubled the value of what you gave me.

Master: Excellent, Secundus, excellent! You are a good and faithful servant. I shall now put you in charge of more of my affairs. We also must celebrate together! Tertius step forward and give an account of what you have done.

Tertius: Master, I know that you are a hard man who harvests where he didn't sow and I was afraid of losing your money. But I thought of a good idea, I buried it in the garden so you could have it all back safe and sound when you returned. Here it is.

Tertius holds up a bag filled with coins to give to the Master

Master: What! I can't believe how lazy you've been! You say I'm a man who harvests where he hasn't sown and you dare to bring back what I gave you without increase! You could have put it on deposit where it would have gained some interest! Crescens, you take his money! I want you all to understand that those of you who use well that which has been given to you will be given even more! Secundus throw this wretch Tertius out he has no place in my home. I tell you the truth; those that are unfaithful will have what little they have taken from them.

Unknown Journey

(Based upon Scripture Genesis 12:1-5)

Characters: **2 camels**

Stage: **Single level**

Scene: **Abram's backyard in Haran**

1ˢᵗ Camel: Are you ready?

2ⁿᵈ Camel: Ready for what?

1ˢᵗ Camel: Not long now and we're all in for a rather long journey!

2ⁿᵈ Camel: Who told you?

1ˢᵗ Camel: That donkey over there.

2ⁿᵈ Camel: You don't want to believe a word he says.

1ˢᵗ Camel: Why?

2ⁿᵈ Camel: He's a bit of an ass!

1ˢᵗ Camel: But he's a pedigree donkey!

2ⁿᵈ Camel: Then he's a complete ass!

1ˢᵗ Camel: Ok! If you don't want to know, I'll tell somebody else.

2ⁿᵈ Camel: Come on what did he say?

1ˢᵗ Camel: Shan't tell you, I'm off!

2ⁿᵈ Camel: Look, don't take the hump!

1ˢᵗ Camel: Now who's talking! I wouldn't tell you if you were the last camel in the yard!

2ⁿᵈ Camel: But I am the last camel in the yard!

1ˢᵗ Camel: Are you?

2ⁿᵈ Camel: Go ahead, not including yourself how many camels are in the yard?

1ˢᵗ Camel: One!

2ⁿᵈ Camel: Satisfied?

1ˢᵗ Camel: Let me double check. One!

2ⁿᵈ Camel: My father always said you couldn't chew cud and walk at the same time.

1ˢᵗ Camel: That does it good and proper! There's no way I'm telling you.

2ⁿᵈ Camel: But there's nobody else to tell.

1ˢᵗ Camel: It doesn't make any difference, my lips are sealed!

2ⁿᵈ Camel: No they're not, you're dribbling!

1ˢᵗ Camel: Do you go out of your way to be rude?

2ⁿᵈ Camel: No, I find I can be rude right here!

1st Camel:	I don't know why I stay here, I really don't!
2nd Camel:	Probably because you're tied up, like me. Now come on. You can't leave me, I can't leave you, so why not tell me your news?
1st Camel:	Well all right, but no poking fun.
2nd Camel:	Ok!
1st Camel:	The donkey told me that he had heard from one of the oxen, who knows a couple of sheep that the sheepdog said…
2nd Camel:	This isn't a shaggy dog story is it?
1st Camel:	No it isn't! Now be quiet or I won't tell you. As I was saying the donkey said…
2nd Came:	Please can we skip the prologue and get to the action?
1st Camel:	All right, the sheepdog overheard Abram speaking to the head shepherd. He was telling him to prepare for a long journey.
2nd Camel:	Perhaps he was giving him the sack!
1st Camel:	No he wasn't because Abram was giving instructions on how he wanted the herds moved when they started on the journey.
2nd Camel:	So where are we going?
1st Camel:	Now that's the interesting part. Abram told the shepherd that God had told him to leave his home and go to the land that he would show him.
2nd Camel:	And where's that?
1st Camel:	He didn't tell him!
2nd Camel:	He didn't tell him?
1st Camel:	He didn't tell him!
2nd Camel:	But we're still all going on this journey?
1st Camel:	Even though we don't know where we're going!
2nd Camel:	And they call us dumb animals!
1st Camel:	But Abram said that God had given him a promise. God said he will bless him and bless everybody in the whole earth if he obeyed.
2nd Camel:	You have to admire Abram in a way. It must take a lot of bottle to leave the home you know and travel into the unknown.
1st Camel:	That's what bothers me. I guess it'll be us that will end up carrying the bottles!

Harvest-time

(Based upon Genesis 8:22)

Characters: **2 camels**

Stage: **Single level**

Scene: **Outside**

1st Camel: Do you ever wonder where our food comes from?

2nd Camel: No!

1st Camel: Why not?

2nd Camel: What's the point? It won't taste any better or worse for knowing were it comes from.

1st Camel: Don't you think that's a dog in the manger attitude?

2nd Camel: No, more of a camel in a yard point of view. You know my philosophy in life don't you?

1st Camel: No.

2nd Camel: You scratch my hump and I'll scratch yours, no questions asked!

1st Camel: But my hump doesn't itch!

2nd Camel: No, you're missing the point, that's my philosophy.

1st Camel: What is?

2nd Camel: I'll scratch…

1st Camel: No, not all that again! What do you mean?

2nd Camel: If you do me a favour, I'll do one for you but let's each mind our own business!

1st Camel: Isn't that a bit isolationist?

2nd Camel: If I knew what you meant I might agree.

1st Camel: Isn't it only responsible to take a concerned interest in the world around us?

2nd Camel: Go down that track and your lost. Before you know what's happened they'll be knocking at your gate demanding donations for starving Dromedaries in the Sudan, political freedom for Bactrians in Outer Mongolia and the repatriation of camels from Australia!

1st Camel: But you must be interested in where your own food comes from?

2nd Camel: I know where it comes from, it comes from that barn over there and if you don't know that I feel sorry for you.

1st Camel: But it came from somewhere else first!

2nd Camel: Is your life always this complicated?

1st Camel: Our fodder is grown on a farm somewhere.

2nd Camel: So? Whoopee do!

1st Camel: But the farmer had to prepare the land and then sow the seed.

2nd Camel: That's good so he's got employment, my appetite has done him a favour!

1st Camel: But that's not all! Once the farmer sows the seed the seed grows all by itself watered by the rain and warmed by the sun.

2nd Camel: Fascinating!

1st Camel: If there is too much or too little water, or too much or too little sun then the farmer will get a poor crop and we'd go short!

2nd Camel: That's bad, so who sorts it all out to get it right?

1st Camel: The Creator.

2nd Camel: The Creator?

1st Camel: Yes, the farmer sows the seed but it's the Creator who gives the increase.

2nd Camel: How do you know that?

1st Camel: I'm surprised that it's news to you. The Creator has promised that "As long as the earth remains, there will be springtime and harvest, cold and heat, winter and summer, day and night."

2nd Camel: Then that means…

1st Camel: Yes, it means we are all camels in his care!

Victory in Battle

(Based upon 2 Chronicles 14:12-15)

Characters: **2 camels**

Stage: **Single level**

Scene: **A yard in Jerusalem**

1st Camel: How long have you been in Jerusalem then?

2nd Camel: Not long, I'm not a good judge of time.

1st Camel: I'm right though aren't I? You're not from around here are you?

2nd Camel: No, I'm not.

1st Camel: Have I seen you before?

2nd Camel: I don't think so.

1st Camel: Are you always this talkative?

2nd Camel: I just like to hang loose, you know, and chew the cud.

1st Camel: You're certainly not from around here are you? Everybody is uptight in Jerusalem. The place zings, never know what's going to happen next.

2nd Camel: Is that right?

1st Camel: Yes! One moment you're chewing the cud in Jerusalem the next minute it's off to fight invading Ethiopians. Are you sure I've not seen you before?

2nd Camel: Like you said, I'm not from around here.

1st Camel: Have you moved around a bit then? You know the old desert drifter thing?

2nd Camel: You could say that.

1st Camel: I just did.

2nd Camel   And without practice! Cool!

1st Camel: Look we're not getting very far here.

2nd Camel: I'm doing fine, I just want to chill!

1st Camel: Gerar!

2nd Camel: I beg you pardon?

1st Camel: It was Gerar, that's where I saw you! You were captured at Gerar. You served with the Ethiopian army.

2nd Camel: I wasn't given any option.

1st Camel: That's ok, say no more, we're both camels of the world.

2nd Camel: Is that it, end of conversation?

1st Camel:	Well there's nothing much left to say is there?
2nd Camel:	You should never have won.
1st Camel:	Why not? True we were playing at home but it was a level desert and a fair result.
2nd Camel:	We should have crushed you!
1st Camel:	Ok! Ok! But stay cool. Some of the lads said that you had a big army.
2nd Camel:	We must have outnumbered you at least two to one!
1st Camel:	So it wasn't what you'd call a fair fight then?
2nd Camel:	You should have eaten our dirt!
1st Camel:	Well I hope you don't mean what I think you mean!
2nd Camel:	How could we have lost?
1st Camel:	It was inevitable.
2nd Camel:	How was it inevitable? We had more warriors, more horses, more chariots, more camels…
1st Camel:	And no Lord.
2nd Camel:	Of course we had a Lord! Zerah was famed throughout North Africa…
1st Camel:	I don't mean a human Lord. We have King Asa but we don't put our trust in him. We put our trust in the Lord God.
2nd Camel:	Don't tell me you believe in all that God stuff! That's for camels with slack humps and weak brains.
1st Camel:	How do you explain that when we in Israel follow our God faithfully we always win against the biggest odds?
2nd Camel:	Perhaps you get lucky!
1st Camel:	Lucky against the Egyptians, the Amalekites, the Assyrians, the Canaanites, the Ethiopians…
2nd Camel:	Ok, you've made your point. May be you're just good fighters!
1st Camel:	We are but when we disobey our Lord God the weakest force can defeat us.
2nd Camel:	Are you having me on?
1st Camel:	No, if we are anything it's because when we obey God he protects us, strengthens us and gives us the victory. All the glory goes to him.

Before the Flood

(Based upon Genesis 6:9-22, 2 Peter 2:5)

Characters: **2 camels**

Stage: **Single level**

Scene: **In a town square before the flood**

1ˢᵗ Camel: Hello! Are you new around here?

2ⁿᵈ Camel: Yes, just visiting.

1ˢᵗ Camel: Where do you live?

2ⁿᵈ Camel: About half a day's journey east from here.

1ˢᵗ Camel: Not far then?

2ⁿᵈ Camel: No, not far. What do you do?

1ˢᵗ Camel: To tell the truth not a lot. Well things have changed around here.

2ⁿᵈ Camel: How do you mean?

1ˢᵗ Camel: The time was when my master felt he could leave his family in safety and make journeys away from home to visit distant relatives and do a bit of trading on the side. It was all right; we used to visit some lovely oases on the way. It was good, nothing too rushed, but we don't do it any more.

2ⁿᵈ Camel: Why not?

1ˢᵗ Camel: It's the violence. The last time we made a trip my master's place was raided, so my master doesn't like staying away any more. They beat up one of his sons and stole a very good friend of mine.

2ⁿᵈ Camel: I'm sorry to hear that.

1ˢᵗ Camel: It was a nasty business, my friend ended up at the local Sizzling Sands Steak Bar and Fast Food Outlet.

2ⁿᵈ Camel: On deliveries?

1ˢᵗ Camel: No, on the menu, he was an ox. It was a nasty business.

2ⁿᵈ Camel: In a funny way I'm here because of your friend. My master is very concerned about all the violence and wickedness that's around.

1ˢᵗ Camel: What does he do?

2ⁿᵈ Camel: He's got a couple of projects on at the moment.

1ˢᵗ Camel: Is that why you're here then?

2ⁿᵈ Camel: Yes, one of his projects is to tell people about the right way to live. You know, how the Creator wants them to live dealing fairly with each other, not fighting to get their own way, putting other people before

	themselves, being kind and considerate and helping those in need.
1st Camel:	I think my master would agree with all that.
2nd Camel:	To be honest he'd be the exception. Nearly everybody laughs at what my master says. Sometimes they throw rocks at him and tell him to clear off!
1st Camel:	What's his other project?
2nd Camel:	He's a boat builder, you know those wooden things that float on water.
1st Camel:	No, you've got me on that one, never seen one. So you live near lots of water then?
2nd Camel:	No, like I said we're half a day's journey to the east of here. There's no water there to float a boat.
1st Camel:	But you said your master is a boat builder?
2nd Camel:	To tell the truth he's building one boat. I reckon it'll take 120 years to finish.
1st Camel:	So he's not up for early retirement then?
2nd Camel:	No! Mark you it is a big boat. A very big boat. Quite huge in fact.
1st Camel:	So, let me get this clear. Your master is building a very big boat where there is no water to float it.
2nd Camel:	That's right!
1st Camel:	Bit of a dafty is he? Two packs short of a load?
2nd Camel:	He says that the Creator told him to build it.
1st Camel:	Does your master talk to the trees as well?
2nd Camel:	There's no need to be offensive. He believes that the Creator is going to destroy the whole earth with a flood to sweep away all the wickedness.
1st Camel:	That's a bit heavy duty isn't it?
2nd Camel:	How many more do you want see end up on the Sizzling Sands Steak Bar menu? Sin is the number one problem on earth because every other problem is a direct result of people sinning. Men are just too proud to admit the Creator knows best.

Tough to be Toast

(Based upon 2 Peter 3:5-10)

Characters: **2 camels**

Stage: **Single level**

Scene: **Mount Ararat**

1st Camel: It's good to get some fresh air after all that time cooped up! We seemed to have been in that thing for ages!

2nd Camel: And a good job that we were. Just look around you!

1st Camel: What a wasteland! Where have all the forests gone?

2nd Camel: Where have all the camels gone?

1st Camel: But look at the ground, everywhere you look there's the fresh green of new shoots.

2nd Camel: Well, the sky is blue and the ground is dry so we can go off into this brand new world. In which direction shall we go?

1st Camel: Down.

2nd Camel: Being at the top of a mountain we can only go down. I meant which side of the mountain shall we go down?

1st Camel: Which way are the tigers going?

2nd Camel: They are going other there!

1st Camel: Which way are the lions going?

2nd Camel: They are going that way!

1st Camel: In that case I don't think we should go over there or that way. Instead why don't we go down the same direction as the giraffes?

2nd Camel: Sounds good to me!

1st Camel: Do you think this'll work?

2nd Camel: What'll work?

1st Camel: This new age, the post-diluvian earth.

2nd Camel: The post-diluvian earth?

1st Camel: Yes, post-diluvian earth, the age after the flood.

2nd Camel: Then I am a post-diluvian camel!

1st Camel: We are both post-diluvian camels!

2nd Camel: It has a certain ring about it, don't you think?

1st Camel: Yes, but it isn't very exclusive is it? Everything we see is post-diluvian!

2nd Camel: What shall we do after we get off this mountain?

1ˢᵗ Camel: You know our instructions, we've got to multiply!

2ⁿᵈ Camel: Trouble is I'm not very good at multiplying.

1ˢᵗ Camel: You should have said so before you got on board.

2ⁿᵈ Camel: Once I get beyond 4 I get really stuck.

1ˢᵗ Camel: What are you talking about?

2ⁿᵈ Camel: Multiplying, I'm not very good at numbers.

1ˢᵗ Camel: You don't have to be, it's not that sort of multiplying. We have got to have baby camels, lots of them. When they grow up they will have baby camels and so on until the world is full of camels!

2ⁿᵈ Camel: I have a distinct feeling of déjà vu about all that.

1ˢᵗ Camel: Come again?

2ⁿᵈ Camel: We've been through all that before, why do we have to do it all again?

1ˢᵗ Camel: Basically because man screwed up! If people had got their act together and obeyed the Creator instead of themselves none of us would have been bobbing around for months in that wooden box.

2ⁿᵈ Camel: What's their problem?

1ˢᵗ Camel: I think it's because they don't chew the cud. It's difficult to get angry when you chew the cud and if you do…

2ⁿᵈ Camel: You choke!

1ˢᵗ Camel: Exactly! Then of course they love to dominate. Once they've got us camels back in harness along with the horses, oxen, donkeys and the rest, they'll turn on each other again, like they did before.

2nd Camel: If that's so why has the Creator given them a second chance?

1ˢᵗ Camel: That's him all over, he loves people. He wants to give them time to come to their senses and follow him.

2ⁿᵈ Camel: So you reckon this flood thing was like a second chance for man to get his act together?

1ˢᵗ Camel: Yes but one thing's for sure, the Creator may be patient but there'll come a time when no time is left to straighten out and sharpen up!

2ⁿᵈ Camel: Why is that?

1ˢᵗ Camel: The Creator has said that the earth will be burnt up by fire on the day of judgement.

2ⁿᵈ Camel: But what about those who don't know God?

1ˢᵗ Camel: They'll be toast!

Easter

(Based upon the Gospels)

Characters: 1 rabbit and 1 girl

Stage: Single level

Scene: Outdoors

A little girl comes up to a rabbit in the park, which is wearing dark glasses.

Girl: Hey Mister Rabbit!

Rabbit: Mister Rabbit! I like that! Thank you for the respect little lady.

Girl: Mister Rabbit, where do you keep your eggs, your Easter eggs?

Rabbit: Do I look like a bird? Do I look like a dude who's into chocolate?

Girl: Hey Mister Rabbit, I said where do you keep your Easter eggs? Come on Mister Rabbit, You are the Easter Bunny, aren't you?

Rabbit: Little girl there is no such thing as the Easter Bunny and even if there was, I would most defi-nate-ly not want the job!

Girl: Don't say that! You must be the Easter Bunny. You're big, you're furry and you wear shades like all the famous people.

Rabbit: Honey, I may be big, I may be furry, I may wear shades, but I ain't no Easter Bunny! Furthermore the Easter Bunny is not real!

Girl: He is too!

Rabbit: He ain't not! Little girl, have you any idea what Easter is about?

Girl: Yes! It's a real cool time when the Easter Bunny comes with chocolate eggs.

Rabbit: You are wrong, wrong, wrong!

Girl: *Angrily.* No I'm not!

Rabbit: Tell me do you think that the Easter Bunny would know what Easter was all about?

Girl: Of course he would.

Rabbit: And you think I'm the Easter Bunny?

Girl: You know you're the Easter Bunny. You're just teasing me.

Rabbit: So, I know all about Easter?

Girl: If you don't who would?

Rabbit:	OK! This is the truth about Easter, the whole truth. Forget about chocolate eggs, forget about the Easter Bunny, forget about fluffy chicks, and forget about daffodils.
Girl:	You're being mean to me! Weren't there even any little lambs?
Rabbit:	There was one lamb.
Girl:	Really?
Rabbit:	Yes, the Lamb of God. God's only son, Jesus, is called the Lamb of God. He came to earth, born like any human baby. He grew up as a good child. When he became a man, he went around doing good things.
Girl:	Like what?
Rabbit:	Like healing people who were sick, giving the blind their sight, the deaf their hearing, the lame and paralysed their mobility, raising the dead and teaching people how God wanted them to live.
Girl:	That sounds really cool!
Rabbit:	It was, but the time came when Jesus was betrayed, arrested, beaten up and false charges made against him. Although innocent, he was sentenced to death, died and was buried in a sealed rock tomb.

The little girl begins to cry, rubbing her eyes with her hands

Rabbit:	Don't cry little girl, the story didn't end there. Jesus died for you and people like you, so that all those who believe in him and do what he says can become friends with God.
Girl:	Is that really true?
Rabbit:	It certainly is! You see Jesus didn't stay dead but rose up from his grave. What's more he said that everybody who believes in him and lives like he wants them to, will rise up when they die and go to a special place he's got ready for them in heaven.
Girl:	Wow! Where can I find out about Jesus?
Rabbit:	You need to get a Bible, you can read all about Jesus in that.
Girl:	Have you got a Bible?
Rabbit:	What good's a Bible to me? I'm a rabbit I can't read. I've been created just to hang out and be cool. It's people like you who've been created to be friends of God. You stick to the Bible and Jesus, and leave me to my grass!

Harvest

(Based upon the Mark 4:26-29 & 1 Corinthians 3:6)

Characters: 1 rabbit and 1 farmer

Stage: Single level

Scene: Outdoors

The rabbit, wearing sunglasses is resting when a farmer enters.

Rabbit:	Hi there! How you're doing old man?
Farmer:	*Very surprised.* Who the! What the! Oh my word!
Rabbit:	Are you all right? didn't mean to give you a scare!
Farmer:	You didn't scare me but I was surprised when you spoke. We don't get many talking rabbits in these parts, or many in sunglasses either. As a matter of fact we don't get too many rabbits of any kind around here. Truth to tell, and no offence intended, we regard them as vermin to be "dealt with" on sight!
Rabbit:	Well we're all entitled to our point of view.
Farmer:	Of course we don't waste anything around here. I love pies, especially rabbit pies.
Rabbit:	I can see you do. But could you just be a littler more sensitive?
Farmer:	Why? You're nothing but vermin and should be treated as such!
Rabbit:	Hey Man! Chill! Stay cool! I've not come to eat your corn, I respect what you do. I'm from the city. Have you ever seen a rabbit in shades before?"
Farmer:	No I ain't seen no rabbit in sunglasses before, so what?
Rabbit:	I'm just trying to say I have no intention of hurting your stuff, so why hurt me?
Farmer:	Look here you smart little whatsit! I grow all this corn by myself without help from anyone, and neither you nor anybody else is going to get near it!
Rabbit:	Whoah, you're absolutely wrong!
Farmer:	How do you make that out? Who are you to say I'm wrong?
Rabbit:	Look I'm just a humble creature as dependent upon a good harvest as anybody else but I think you need help to understand some realities.
Farmer:	Realities like what?

Rabbit:	Realities like you never grew those crops all by yourself. You could never do it.
Farmer:	What do you mean?
Rabbit:	This is the way it is. You prepared the ground and planted the seed. But after that God watered it and caused it all to multiply and grow. It's God who's given you your harvest, not your own efforts. If God didn't water the crops and care for them all your work would be for nothing!
Farmer:	Dang me! You're right little vermin! You're right!
Rabbit:	Of course I am! All our food comes to us as a result of God's goodness and that's something to remember as we give thanks for it.

Christmas

(Based upon the Gospels)

Characters: 1 rabbit and a little boy

Stage: Single level

Scene: Outdoors

The Rabbit, in sunglasses, is minding its own business when along comes a little boy.

Boy:	Hey! I bet I can tell you where you're from!
Rabbit:	And where's that?
Boy:	You've got white on you like a polar bear or an arctic fox. So you must come from where it's cold and snowy.
Rabbit:	No I'm not, you're a product of too much education for your years!
Boy:	But I know all about camouflage. You've got white on you because you live in the snow! Furthermore, I bet you know Santa Claus!
Rabbit:	No way! My daddy was black and he didn't live in a coal mine and I don't live in the snow. And as for Santa Claus, he doesn't even exist.
Boy:	*Angrily.* He does exist! My daddy told me and he's bigger than you!
Rabbit:	Most people are but that doesn't mean they or your daddy are right!
Boy:	It does too!
Rabbit:	Has your daddy ever been to where the snow lays thick and heavy and polar bears and arctic foxes do their thing?
Boy:	No, I don't think so.
Rabbit:	So you if you believe that I come from where your daddy has never been, does it not seem reasonable to suppose that I may know just a bit more about where I come from than your daddy does?
Boy:	I'll have to think about that.
Rabbit:	What do you think Christmas is all about?
Boy:	That's easy! It's about Santa Claus, decorating the house, getting presents and eating all sorts of good stuff.
Rabbit:	Would you like to know why people celebrate Christmas?
Boy:	Yes please.
Rabbit:	A long time ago God had an enemy who turned people away from being friends with God. But God had an idea. He decided to send his only Son to come and destroy all the works of his enemy and show people how to

live lives that would make them happy.

Boy: That sounds like it was a good idea.

Rabbit: It does, doesn't it? Well God's Son came to earth as a little baby born to a young lady sheltering with her husband in the stable of a lodging house in a town.

Boy: Where was the town?

Rabbit: It was in a country we know today as Israel. Lots of people had to go to the same town to register for tax purposes, when they ran out of rooms people had to sleep wherever they could.

Boy: Did people know he was God's son when he was born?

Rabbit: Some had a very shrewd idea. An angel came to shepherds out in the fields on the night the baby was born and told them that God's promised Messiah, his Anointed One, had been born that night in their town, Bethlehem. The baby's mother must have thought it strange when wise men came to see the baby and worshiped him because you shouldn't worship anyone but God.

Boy: What was the baby called?

Rabbit: Jesus.

Boy: And did he do all that God wanted him to do?

Rabbit: Every last thing that God wanted him to do he did, he left nothing out.

Boy: Why do we have all the stuff like decorations and presents and food if Christmas is all about getting back to be friends with God?

Rabbit: Man, I'm just a rabbit, like I don't dig turkey, decorations, cake and all that jive. I mean like some things I don't know and humans are one of them. They are just way too complicated for me to understand. Just lead me to the cool grass and I have all I need.

Boy: But where can I find out more about Christmas?

Rabbit: If you get a Bible you can read all about it for yourself. Share it with whoever you can and, whether they accept it or not, don't you ever forget that Jesus came so you could be friends with God!

God Is There!

(Based upon Psalm 53:1)

Characters: **1 rabbit and 1 man**

Stage: **Single level**

Scene: **Outdoors**

The rabbit is resting in the park in sunglasses when a man comes by

Rabbit: What a lovely day to stretch out in the shade!

Man: My O my! A talking rabbit!

Rabbit: Hey buster! Can you hop?

Man: Sure I can hop.

Rabbit: Well My O my! A hopping human!

The man's bottom jaw drops and he stares at the rabbit

Rabbit: Pardon me, but I was taught it was rude to stare!

Man: My O my! A talking, educated rabbit!

Rabbit: Do you have a problem with me getting an education?

Man: No, not at all. Why I'm the most educated man I know. I'm for everybody getting the best education they can. It's just that I've not met a talking rabbit before.

Rabbit: Well it's good to talk just as it's good to hop. So I talk, you hop and we can all chill out and be way cool. Tell me, just how well are you educated? What sort of stuff do you know?

Man: Well I guess I pretty well know all there is to know. Why don't you try me out?

Rabbit; Who invented the parachute and when was the first successful jump made?

Man: Leonardo da Vinci invented the parachute in AD 1480 but the first successful jump did not take place until 1912. Do you want another go?

Rabbit: Sure. When and where did the first printed newspaper appear?

Man: I see you like tough questions with a tricky edge. But that question is not too tough for me! The first printed newspaper appeared in Beijing in AD 748. They actually started printing books there in AD 600.

Rabbit: Well how about London, England, when was that founded?

Man: Dead easy, that one! It was founded in AD 43. Is that all, or would you like one more?

Rabbit: OK, when did the Olympic games first take place?

Man: Tricky! There could be two answers to this question. You see it's possible they started in 1350 BC but the first recorded games took place in 748 BC. They featured horse racing, pentathlon, wrestling, boxing and running.

Rabbit: Before you go, what's all this AD/BC stuff with the dates?

Man: It's simple, BC stands for Before Christ and AD for Anno Domini, which is Latin for in the year of Our Lord. As the calendar developed in Western Europe the date of the birth of Jesus Christ was taken as pivotal to the history of the world, so everything was dated from before and after his birth.

Rabbit: So who was this Jesus then?

Man: Oh just some middle-eastern itinerant teacher who got a following. Some said he was the Son of God, but as there is no God that does not seem likely!

Rabbit: Whoah! Hold on man! You mean to say you don't believe in a God!

Man: That's right! Any rational educated person, and I daresay rabbit, can see that to believe in some Supreme Being is merely a comfort to those of a lesser intellect.

The rabbit begins to laugh uncontrollably

Man: Why are you laughing?

Rabbit: Man, I'm laughing because you who set yourself up to be so wise have just proved you're a fool!

Man: *Angrily* How dare you insult my great intelligence!

Rabbit: Man it's not I who insult you but you've condemned yourself out of your own mouth. The Bible says that the fool has said in his heart that there is no God. So I guess that makes you a fool! Have a nice day!

Creation

(Based upon Genesis 1 and 2)

Characters: **1 rabbit and 1 man**

Stage: **Single level**

Scene: **Outdoors**

The rabbit meets a man standing at a viewpoint in the country

Rabbit: Good morning! Wonderful view isn't it?

Man: I beg your pardon?

Rabbit: I said, "Wonderful view isn't it?"

Man: I know you did but I know you can't talk. You see I'm a scientist.

Rabbit: Well, nobody would know unless you told them.

Man: No the point I'm making is that biologically, it's impossible for you to talk. Evolution has not equipped rabbits with the necessary equipment.

Rabbit: What's evolution?

Man: Rabbits evolved from primitive creatures millions of years ago. Your ancestors were most likely amphibians that crawled out of primeval slime.

Rabbit: Man, that don't seem at all right to me! Let me make it clear, us rabbits do not like slime, primeval or otherwise. You don't get no sweet vibes through your whiskers if they're clogged up with mud and stuff.

Man: Let's take this one step, or I should say, one hop at a time, old chap. At the beginning of the world there was a cocktail of chemicals that produced the elements necessary for life, such as carbon and hydrogen.

Rabbit: May I ask a question? Who made the world?

Man: Oh, it's not a who, it was an event; probably a spontaneous cosmic explosion.

Rabbit: I thought explosions destroyed things, not created them!

Man: The explosion created a chemical reaction that resulted in planet earth and a whole lot more besides!

Rabbit: So where does the slime come into it?

Man: Without making it complicated, different chemicals were created at random and the resultant chance combinations eventually produced primitive life forms. As millennia went by these evolved into more

	complex organisms, until the present day.
Rabbit:	So, how did eyes develop?
Man:	What eyes?
Rabbit:	Your eyes, my eyes, how did they evolve?
Man:	I'm not sure.
Rabbit:	Why aren't you sure?
Man:	The mechanism by which the eyes of vertebrates evolved would have been that of advantageous mutations, but the precise nature of such mutations is not familiar to me.
Rabbit:	Cool it man! What's that in English? I'm a rabbit, remember? I don't have the advantage of your advanced learning. Man, us rabbits don't even get a literacy hour!
Man:	Basically, it's thought that evolution from simple organisms to complex life forms took place through a series of chance changes that proved to be beneficial. So these changes or mutations came to be passed on, so that life forms evolved to become what they are today. I trust that that is clear enough?
Rabbit:	Let's just take this real slow. You've just described creation through chaos. According to you, there's no plan involved just chance. But every time I take a walk in the park I see harmony, I see a design, I see a plan.
Man:	You, my friend, are a rabbit. Since when have rabbits been a sound source of scientific theory?
Rabbit:	I am simply saying that the created world we see around us is the product of a rational and loving mind. It is true that pollution by your kind has fouled the seas and rivers and tainted the air. However, left to itself there is a rhythm and harmony to nature that suggests thought and care in its creation, not chance and mutation.
Man:	I see no purpose in continuing a conversation with a closed mind!
Rabbit:	One last thing before you go. How come a bright dude like you can't see God's signature in creation?

God Uses Animals!

(Based upon 1 Kings 17:4, 2 Kings 2:24, Numbers 22:28-30, Jonah 1 and 2, Matthew 17:27)

Characters: **1 rabbit and 1 woman**

Stage: **Single level**

Scene: **Outdoors in a Park**

The rabbit meets a "hippie" woman standing in a park meditating

Rabbit: Hi there! You sure look cool in all those beads.

The woman turns to face the rabbit and faints. The rabbit bends down.

Rabbit: Hey! Lady, it's OK, I'm not going to hurt you.

Woman: *Staggering to her feet covering her eyes.* It's far out, I thought you were a rabbit!

Rabbit: Open your eyes, lady. I am a rabbit!

Woman: But you can talk!

Rabbit: Kind of neat isn't it? I'm the only rabbit in town who can go to the pet store and order his own food. Although I love to come and sample the cool grass in the park.

Woman: So do I!

Rabbit: What were you doing before I interrupted you?

Woman: I was tuning in to the vibes of the trees. They talk to me you know.

Rabbit: Yeah sure, lady. The trees talk to you. I've never noticed that they've had much to say.

Woman: Oh, they say so much to me. They love me.

Rabbit: Right! How do you know they love you?

Woman: They envelop me in their fragrance, they watch over me, shielding me from the harsh rays of the sun. Stand with me and let them talk to you.

The woman stares upward arms outstretched, the rabbit looks around

Rabbit: Sorry! I guess they're not talking today.

Woman: Oh but they are! Listen, hear them now! Tell me you hear them.

Rabbit: Lady, all I can hear is the wind rustling the leaves. You know trees can't talk.

Woman: *Angrily.* That is ridiculous! Why nobody has ever heard of a talking animal, but you talk.

Rabbit:	Let's not argue about this. But I have to tell you that there is a record of an animal speaking, which has been known for centuries.
Woman:	I've never heard of it, where can I learn about it?
Rabbit:	The animal was an ass owned by a man called Balaam in the Bible.
Woman:	And did this ass speak all the time?
Rabbit:	Not that I know of. The man was riding off to do some dirty work against God's people. God sent an angel into his path but he couldn't see it. However, his ass did and she saved his life when she refused to go pass the angel. The man beat his donkey and that's when she spoke to him.
Woman:	That's some story, is it true?
Rabbit:	Yes it's true Lady, I know what God can do through us animals. Why, he sent a big fish to redirect his prophet Jonah to Nineveh. Then he had ravens feed another prophet called Elijah. When youths insulted yet another prophet called Elisha, God sent two bears to sort them out! And when Jesus and Peter needed to pay tax God sent a fish with the money.
Woman:	So there is a God after all?
Rabbit:	Lady, the Bible says that God made the animals as well as people. The Bible also shows that God cares for them. Why, Jesus himself said that his heavenly Father feeds the birds of the air.
Woman:	Have you read all this up yourself?
Rabbit:	Lady, I'm a rabbit and rabbits can't read. But you can read it all for yourself. Then instead of trying to hear the trees talk, you would hear God speaking to you through his word, which would be a whole lot better! If God cares for us animals he surely cares for you. It's time you got to know him!